LETTING GO

LINDA ESTES

Energion Publications
Gonzalez, FL
2018

Blessings
Linda

e-books:
Kindle: 978-1-63199-493-7
Adobe Digital Editions: 978-1-63199-492-0
iBooks: 978-1-63199-494-4
Google Play: 978-1-63199-495-1

Print:
ISBN10: 1-63199-616-9
ISBN13: 978-1-63199-616-0
Library of Congress Control Number: 2018961516

Energion Publications
P. O. Box 841
Gonzalez, FL 32560
850-525-3916

energion.com
pubs@energion.com

INTRODUCTION - LETTING GO

This book starts and ends with a couple of verses that have become near and dear to my heart, Ephesians 3:20-21.

Now to Him who is able to do far more abundantly beyond all that we ask or think, according to the power that works within us, to Him be the glory in the church and in Christ Jesus to all generations forever and ever. Amen.

There were lots of things that died with Alan when he passed away over two years ago. Lots of dreams and plans we had in our heads and held in our hearts. Letting go of all of those things was hard, gut-wrenchingly hard. But just like those verses say, God has done more than I could even dream of or imagine after I was willing to let go of them. Here's one example.

Alan was going to breed the horse that he rode to a jack so I could experience a foal. Well, that was a dream I had to let go, or so I thought. You see, we had five horses at our place when Alan died unexpectedly. Knowing I couldn't take care of them, I found them new homes. It was hard, but sometimes life is just like that. The horses weren't the only things that I couldn't take care of. I had to have others help me with maintaining the farm. After a year of others helping, I began to realize that there was more that I was going to have to let go of. The Lord helped me little by little to let go of things I no longer needed or could manage: household items, farm equipment … "stuff."

Then as another year neared the end, God asked me to give up something I was not ready to give up, the home Alan and I shared. It didn't make sense to me that the Lord would ask me to let go of a perfectly good home where so many beautiful memories and hopeful dreams were shared, yet the Lord was making it clear to me that He was asking me to let go of it. However, He didn't just make it clear that I was to leave our home; He made a way. Through nearly a two-year process, in His perfect timing, God helped me let go. Once I did, everything started moving quickly. From the time I verbalized that I was willing to let go of the farm until God led me to find my new house, close on it, and move in -- was less than two weeks. That's fast ... that was God!

When I moved into my new house in May of 2018, the Lord blessed me beyond all that I could ask or think of, just like Ephesians 3:20-21 talks about. In the field behind the backyard of my new house were horses! Not just full-grown horses, but foals, too! And not just one horse, but 22 horses, including 10 foals!!! Alan wanted me to experience the babies, and God saw to it that I did. Here's the best part. I can love on those horses and feed them carrots at the fence and then when I'm finished, I can go inside. I have all the benefits without the cost or responsibility that goes along with owning horses. At our farm, I had to go outside if I wanted to see the horses and call them up from the field to the barn lot. But at my new house, I can see them even when I'm inside. From my kitchen window ... horses. From my dining room windows ... horses. And from my living room and bedroom windows ... horses!

But in order to receive this blessing from the Lord, I had to let go of something I loved, our home and our farm. Only then could the Lord bless me beyond what I could ever have imagined. When I was thinking and praying about what I wanted in my new house, horses were never on the list. I never dreamed they could be. Only God knew how much my heart ached over having to find new homes for our horses after Alan died. Even though I knew it was something that needed to be done, it still broke my heart to let go of them. When I moved into my new house it was as if God was saying, "Daughter, these horses are My gift to you." The Lord not only provided for all of my needs with my new home, but He also gave me something that I dearly loved, and those horses are my daily reminder that letting go of whatever God asks of me is always in my best interest. I might not understand the "why"

 behind it, but I know that God knows me better than I know myself and He cares about every single detail in my life. Every day God is wanting to show me something new through the writing of these daily devotions. Even though letting go has been hard, He has been right there with me, guiding and directing

my steps. My prayer is that as you read these daily devotions, they will help you trust God more so that when He asks you to let go of something, even if it doesn't immediately make sense, you will say yes to His request.

Love and prayers, Linda

1...USING GOD'S EXTINGUISHER

Good morning! The other night I was sitting outside on my patio with a girlfriend talking about a situation of one person constantly trying to make life difficult for another person and whether we could do anything to stop the instigator. My train of thought got interrupted by a mosquito that bit me. I fixed that problem by putting on my fire pit. With that on, there were no more bugs bothering us. As we talked, and I watched the flames, a couple of things came to mind. First, there are many people out there that are just like the mosquitoes ... a pest, a nuisance, but only for a short time. And then there are those who let the enemy use them to throw fiery arrows at us. We all know how to handle mosquitoes but how do we handle the second kind of difficult person?

Ephesians 6:16 says, "...In addition to all, taking up the shield of faith with which you will be able to extinguish all the flaming arrows of the evil one." There are so many things I love about this verse. First of all, we are given a SHIELD OF FAITH through the power and authority of Jesus Christ. The Lord doesn't just leave us hanging out there to try and fend off people that want to hurt us. Second, I love that with this shield of faith, we are given the power through Jesus to extinguish ALL the flaming arrows of the evil one. I'm so glad that the Lord didn't say, "Here are a dozen, one-time uses for your shield. Use them wisely." Again, the Lord doesn't leave us hanging. He has provided us the Shield of Faith to use whenever fiery arrows come our way, with no limit on the number of uses. And third, I love the fact that the Lord says that those shields will EXTINGUISH all the flames. Not slow them down or deflect them off us for now, but to totally put them out ... extinguish them.

When my girlfriend left, I turned off my fire pit, which totally extinguished the flames. And as I put the lid on the pit, I thanked God for giving us all we need to extinguish the fiery arrows from those that mean us harm.

Lord, help us use the tools that You have so graciously given us. Amen.

2...PUNCH HIM OUT

Good morning! Are you already weighed down today with the troubles and situations in your life? Me too. But recognizing this, we can do something about it. There is nothing more satisfying to the enemy than to render a Christian out for the count, even if it's just for a day. Life can easily be compared to a boxing match. Every new morning, we start out in our perspective corners. As we enter our day, we come out into the center of the ring where the daily battle occurs. Satan will do everything he can to beat us down with his lies, schemes, and deception. He wants to put us in a pit of despair, causing us to retreat, broken and unable to stand strong. The good news is that we don't have to live like this. Psalm 40:1-3 tells us what the Lord will do for us when we find ourselves beaten down in a pit of despair.

> *I waited patiently for the Lord; and He inclined to me and heard my cry. He brought me up out of the pit of destruction, out of the miry clay, and He set my feet upon a rock making my footsteps firm. He put a new song in my mouth, a song of praise to our God; many will see and fear and will trust in the Lord.*

The Lord will hear our cries (our prayers) and pull us out of the pit (center of the ring) and give us a solid rock to stand on (Jesus) so that we won't drop down into the pit that the enemy tries to keep us down in with a 10 count.

But that's only the first part of what this Scripture tells us the Lord will do. Beside rescuing us from the enemy's pit and his hopeful 10 count, which would leave us down and out, the Lord will also put a new song in our heart, a song of praise to our God. With that song of praise coming from our lips, there is no room for any darkness from the enemy, which will render him useless in our lives. If the enemy has you down, remember you are not defeated. Pray the promises that God gives us in these verses in Psalm 40. So, here's to coming out of our corners and punching the enemy in the mouth, leaving him unable to tell his lies, or carry out his schemes.

Heavenly Father, thank You that we can render the enemy useless in our lives through the power of Jesus Christ. Amen.

3...ASK AWAY

Good morning! Do you remember asking your parents for things when you were little? Their answer was usually one of three responses: yes, no, or not now. We loved the "yes" answer, didn't particularly care for the "no" answer, and the "not now" answer gave us a little hope. God usually gives us those same three answers to our prayer requests, but there is a huge difference on how we need to look at His answers.

As a child, because we thought like a child, we couldn't see anything good coming from a "no" answer. As Believers, hopefully we can see that a "no" answer is just as good as a "yes" answer when it comes from God. Just like our parents, He has our best interest at heart. But unlike our parents, who were going with only what they knew at that time, God knows what your whole life looks like. We just have to trust that He has everything under His control. And He does!!

Jesus says in Matthew 7:9-11,

> *"Or what man is there among you, when his son shall ask him for a loaf, will give him a stone? Or if he shall ask for a fish, he will not give him a snake, will he? If you then, being evil, know how to give good gifts to your children, how much more shall your Father who is in heaven give what is good to those who ask him!"*

Did you catch that? God wants to give us "what is good." But He also says that we need to ask Him. Have you ever thought that you might not have something because you never asked for it? Sometimes we don't feel that what we are wanting is important enough to bother God and ask Him for it, so we don't. But our generous Heavenly Father wants to give us what is good. He's just waiting for us to ask!

Heavenly Father, help me understand the answers
You give me are all good, even if Your answer
is NO. And when necessary, remind me Holy
Spirit that nothing is too big or too small to ask
for because You want to be a part of every detail
of my life. Amen.

4...THE GIFT OF TIME

Good morning! I've been reflecting a lot about life since my time in the hospital last week. In our lives, we are only given a set amount of time and there are no "do-overs." I don't know about you, but for me, not many days go by that I don't wish I could have a do-over on something from that day and wished I had more than the twenty-four hours we are given each day.

Are you a list maker? I have been one my whole life. But as one of God's children, I've learned how to deal with my lists better. These days when I look at my list, I asked the Lord to filter my list through His priorities. I'm wanting Him to cross out for me anything that doesn't need to happen and mark those things that are a priority for today. I'm getting pretty good with my lists this way but still get thrown off from time to time with what He adds to my list. This usually requires me to go back to my list and remove something to make room for God's add-on.

I love Psalm 90:12. It's a good verse to use as a prayer when I'm dealing with time issues. "So, teach us to number our days, that we may present to Thee a heart of wisdom." God wants to help us make the most of our time, so we can grow in wisdom. Verse 17 says, "And let the favor of the Lord our God be upon us; and do confirm for us the work of our hands." Just like this verse says, don't we all want the life He's given us to count for Him? We want the work that we do for the Lord to have meaning. As much as we want this, God wants it even more for us. So, as we go about our day, let's focus on the precious resource that God has given us, time, and use it wisely.

Lord, help me to do the things today that would honor You. Since I know that once an hour passes, I'll never get that hour back. So please give me Your guidance in using my time wisely and may my lists reflect Your priorities for me life.
Amen.

5...IT'S BEST MULTIPLIED

Good morning! There is a country song that often pops in my head when I'm reading the words spoken by Jesus in the New Testament. The song is by Brooks & Dunn, entitled "Believe." It was one of Alan's favorite songs. The line of the song I'm referring to says that the old man was "finding more and more truth in the words written in red." I think that statement might be true for all of us as we get older and our perceived time here on earth gets shorter. We pay more attention to the words of Jesus written in our Bible in red.

I learn best when I can see things in my head. I think that is why I love the parables that Jesus told. In Matthew 25:14-30, we read about the parable of talents. As the story goes, a man who was getting ready to take a journey entrusted his possessions to three slaves. To one of them he gave five talents, to another he gave two talents, and to the last one he gave one talent. As the story continues, we learn that by trading, the slave with five talents was able to turn those into 10 talents. And the one that was given two talents doubled his to four talents. But the one given only one talent hid his.

The difference between these three is what they did with what was given to them. We all have "talents" that God gives to us. But what do we do with them? Are we like the first two in this parable? Do we use the gifts God gives us as an extension of His love in serving others, or do we hide our talents and keep what God has given us to ourselves??? Just like in this parable, God blesses those who use and multiply what He has given them. So today, let's be in the "multiplying" business!!

God, You have given us so much through Jesus. Each of us has been given specific talents and gifts. Help us to see exactly what those are and then how we can use them to serve You and others. Amen.

6...ALL IN

Good morning! As we are only a day away from Thanksgiving, I'm sure your schedule is starting to get crazy busy. There are things to get at the grocery store for our Thanksgiving dinners, houses that need to be cleaned for our guests, and traveling that needs to be planned out. We have so much to be thankful for and we tend to be really good at thanking God for all the blessings in our life around Thanksgiving, which is a really good thing.

But as I was reading in Joshua, a question came to mind. Joshua 24:15 tells us to "choose for yourselves today whom you will serve ..." That is a decision that we all need to make every single day of our lives. We can either serve the Creator of heaven and earth or we can serve ourselves via the ways of the world. Since we can't serve them both, and we can't serve them half-and-half either, we must decide between the two. Commitment is one of those things that doesn't seem to be honored much these days, but that's exactly what God requires of us. We need to be 100% committed to following the Lord. That doesn't mean we're not going to still sin and mess up, but hopefully not as much as we used to, and when we do, that we ask for forgiveness much sooner.

So, as we count our many blessings during this time of thanksgiving, let's take a moment to make sure that we have made a commitment to whom we shall serve: God or self. My prayer is that our answer will be the same thing as we find in Joshua 24:15. "But as for me and my house, we will serve the Lord."

Heavenly Father, we are told numerous times in Scripture to be thankful, so we know it's important to You. And since it is important to You, we should be all about it. Help us be mindful of all that we have to be thankful for. With the help of the Holy Spirit, may our praises and thankfulness become as natural to us as breathing. Amen.

7...PRAISE HIM

Good morning! Praying you had a blessed Thanksgiving with your family and friends yesterday and that you took time to reflect on all of the blessings God has given you. Through the pages in the Bible, we can find one reason after another why we should be thankful and praise God for what He's done for us. Today, I camped out in Psalm 111. In these ten verses, the psalmist is encouraging us to praise the Lord and he gives us three good reasons why we should.

The first one is that we should be thankful for all the ways God shows us His power. We can look at nature and see it everywhere. If you've ever been to the ocean, it's easy to see that there could be no other explanation other than it had to be God's great power at work to command the water to stop when it reached the land.

The second reason we should praise God is because He's always taking care of our needs. Even when life throws us for a loop, we can look past that problem and see that God is still providing for us everything that we need, like food, clothing, and a place to lay our head at night.

But the most important reason that we should praise God, is for His gift of salvation. Have you ever given much thought to the fact that if we didn't have Jesus, we wouldn't be able to have a relationship with God? Since nothing unholy (aka...us) could be in the presence of the holy God, we'd be out of luck. Without the Lord, we would have no hope. But thankfully, we do have hope through Jesus. My prayer for us is that we would never look past all the blessings God has given us, and that each and every minute, of each and every day, we would continuously praise Him!

Lord, help us to see the countless ways that You bless us daily. May we always have Your praises on our lips. Amen.

8...JUST PASSING THROUGH

Good morning! I have been blessed with such a good family. On Sunday, my brother and sister in-law stopped by my place on their way back home to the St. Louis area. The visit and lunch were really nice, but it's what happened after lunch that was incredible. They gave my house a face lift by flipping two rooms. They took the furniture from the living room and put it in the family room and vice versa. Switching the furniture has given my house a brand new look. It's amazing!

This morning as I sit here enjoying this room change, I was reminded of another thing about heaven that I'm excited to see one day. In John 14:2, Jesus says, "In My Father's house are many dwelling places; if it were not so, I would have told you; for I go to prepare a place for you." Don't you just love the fact that Jesus, who was a carpenter here on earth, is preparing a dwelling place for us in heaven? Can you imagine what it will look like, especially knowing that we are going to get to our heavenly home by walking on streets of gold? I don't think we've seen anything close to the beauty we will experience there.

As Christians, our forever home is in Heaven. We are just passing through here on earth. But while we are here, we can still keep our focus on heavenly things. Just like a family get-together, you want everyone to be able to come, so our job here is to tell everyone that we can about the home that is waiting for every Believer in Heaven. The gift of salvation not only secures us a home in Heaven but gives us many advantages while we are living here. Once we accept the gift of salvation, we have Jesus by our side from that day forth and the Holy Spirit is our constant companion to guide us through each day. So, here's to helping others see that "there's no place like home!"

Lord, our hearts long to be in heaven with You.
But until the day that You bring us home, let our
lives be focused on bringing others home with
us by telling them about the gift of salvation.
Amen.

9...RUN THAT RACE

Good morning! As I sit here doing my morning devotion, I am reminded of a verse that has helped me get through the tough times. This verse is on a picture that hangs in my living room. Hebrews 12:1 reminds me to keep pushing on. "Let us run with endurance the race God has set before us."

In this verse, we are told to run with endurance. Our journey in life is more of a marathon than a sprint. Endurance is when we "cowgirl up" and don't give in to the situation and let God help us take another step. Sometimes, it's just taking that first step that we need help with, and other times we need help on the hundredth step, and yet other times we need help for every step. You get the idea.

In my life I have found that venting to someone that I trust about my situation helps me get things off my chest. When I hang onto things and don't get them off my chest, that's when the enemy likes to come in and mess with me. He would like nothing more than for me to keep chewing on the same thing over and over because he knows that gets my focus off God and squarely on whatever the situation is.

The best way to not fixate on the problem is to realize what the last line of that verse says..."the race God has set before us." When I acknowledge the fact that whatever is happening in my life, it is there because God has set it before me, my mindset changes. I must remember that God has either orchestrated the situation or has allowed it to be in my life. Since He has placed it before me, He will be with me in whatever it is. And as long as God is with me, I can endure anything because I am never alone. My prayer is that you also take God with you as you run the race He has set before you.

God, with You by my side, there isn't any part of the race out there that I can't run. Thank you for Your constant help. Amen.

10...REASON FOR MY HOPE

Good morning! As I finished wrapping Christmas presents for this year, I stopped to thank God for giving me the means to get out and buy these gifts for those I love. But as I was thinking about all the gifts God has given me, I was once again reminded that the things in life that mean the most can't be bought. Those things are like the gift of time, memories, family traditions, everyday kindnesses, and genuine love.

Have you noticed that the holidays seem to either bring out the best in people or their worst? I think we see less than their best due to the stress that often comes with the "to do" lists that we create during these times. I don't know why we make things so complicated. It seems that the simpler we can make holidays, the more we enjoy them. When we are not stressed out, we can enjoy the time God has given us with family and friends. We can make new and lasting memories and can enjoy those family traditions that warm our hearts. And when our hearts are warmed, everyday kindnesses just naturally flow from us to others.

Our best example of genuine love comes straight from the Lord. 1 Peter 3:15 says, "But sanctify Christ as Lord in your hearts, always being ready to make a defense to everyone who asks you to give an account for the hope that is in you, yet with gentleness and reverence..." Or in other words, we need to be ready to share the hope we have through Jesus in a loving way any time we are asked. The question we could get asked could be something like, "How can you stay so positive with everything going on in your life?" And that's when we can share our faith by telling them that the only way we could still be positive is because we're not doing this life alone. Jesus is with us every step of the way. Praying you'll have your answer ready when asked to give the reason for your hope.

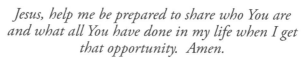

Jesus, help me be prepared to share who You are and what all You have done in my life when I get that opportunity. Amen.

11...PLEASING TO GOD

Good morning! At church on Sunday, my pastor talked about one of the people we read about in the Bible, Enoch. When I get to heaven, Enoch is one of those people I want to find and have a conversation with. But until the Lord takes me to heaven, I want to live like Enoch because he lived a life pleasing to the Lord. I'm sure it was clear to others that he was living like he was loved! In Hebrews 11:5, we find testimony of Enoch's triumph of faith. "By faith Enoch was taken up so that he would not see death; and he was not found because God took him up; for he obtained the witness that before his being taken up he was pleasing to God."

Very little information is given to us about Enoch but Genesis 5:23-24 gives us a tad bit more. "So, all the days of Enoch were three hundred and sixty-five years. Enoch walked with God; and he was not, for God took him." Wow, can you imagine living for that long? As hard as that is to picture, the picture of Enoch talking to God as he was taking a Sunday stroll through the park here on earth (the strolling through the park is my visual, not scriptural) AND then instantly walking in Heaven with Him is mind-boggling. Enoch did not have to experience death and I'm all in favor of that!!

How do we live a life that is pleasing to God? The Bible is our guide in life. Through the pages from Genesis to Revelations we read about those things that please God. But it all starts with faith as Hebrews 11:6 tells us. "And without faith it is impossible to please Him, for he who comes to God must believe that He is and that He is a rewarder of those who seek Him." So, the first question that needs to be answered is have you placed your faith in Jesus? If so, Hallelujah! If not, I pray today would be the day you'd put your trust in the Lord.

Lord, help us be more like Enoch and live a life that would be pleasing to You. Help us as we seek to learn more about You. Amen.

12...HE SET ME FREE

Good morning! "And the truth shall set you free" is a phrase most of us have heard many times, but did you know that it is more than a common phrase? It's actually Scripture. We find it in John 8:32 through Jesus' own words. "... and you shall know the truth, and the truth shall make you free." You know, sometimes life is just messy. We want to live in perfect harmony, but that's not always the case. We want everyone to just be nice and kind, but that doesn't always happen either. And then you turn on the news and wonder what's wrong with people. Sometimes we just want someone to answer the question, "How did this life get so crazy???"

As I was searching to find the scripture about how truth can set us free, I found the answer to how things got so crazy. Earlier in John 8, a woman was brought to Jesus who had been caught in adultery. The Scribes and the Pharisees said that in the Law Moses had commanded them to stone such a woman. They were testing Jesus to see what He would say. It was in Jesus' response that I found the answer to why everything has gotten so crazy. In verse 7, Jesus said to them, "He who is without sin among you, let him be the first to throw a stone at her." And there's our answer to explain why...sin. We live in a fallen, sinful world, and as a result, things like heartache and disappointment are just a natural byproduct of sin. As the story of the adulteress woman continued, no stones were thrown because none present were without sin. In verse 34 Jesus says, "Truly, truly, I say to you, everyone who commits sin is the slave of sin." Being a slave to sin is true bondage. But the good news is that we don't have to stay in that condition because the truth that sets us free is found in Jesus. When we accept Jesus as our Lord and Savior, believing in who He is and what He did to set us free from the bondage of sin, we are forever freed from the penalty of sin. And when Jesus sets us free, we are free indeed!!

Jesus, thank You for setting me free! Please help me share that freedom with others. Amen.

13...PEACE OF GOD

Good morning! 'Tis the season for "peace on earth and goodwill to men," or at least that's what the songs we sing this time of year say. But is that true? Is there peace on earth? Do we offer goodwill to men? One of those songs we sing directs us to how we obtain peace on earth. The lyrics will probably be familiar to you. "With every step I take, let this be my solemn vow: To take each moment, and live each moment in peace eternally. Let there be peace on earth and let it begin with me." Peace on earth begins with each of us. If we don't have peace, we can't share peace with others.

Lasting peace only comes from our Heavenly Father. Here are three of my favorite verses dealing with peace. John 14:27 says, "Peace I leave with you; My peace I give to you; not as the world gives, do I give to you. Let not your heart be troubled nor let it be fearful." Another verse found in the book of John dealing with peace is John 16:33. "These things I have spoken to you, that in Me you may have peace. In the world you have tribulation but take courage; I have overcome the world." And then there is Philippians 4:6-7. "Be anxious for nothing, but in everything by prayer and supplication with thanksgiving let your requests be made known to God; and the peace of God, which surpasses all comprehension, shall guard your hearts and your minds in Christ Jesus."

Isn't the peace of God what we all want? Even though the world has gotten pretty crazy, these Scriptures remind us that we can still have peace ... God's peace. The peace that passes all understanding can be ours. My prayer for us through this holiday season, and always, is that we all might experience the peace of the Lord. Then we can truly live out the song lyrics ... "Let there be peace on earth and let it begin with me."

God, Your peace is what we all desire, even when
we aren't aware that's what we are looking for.
Allow me to help someone find that peace in You.
Amen.

14...PICNICS

Good morning! As I was covering up this morning with one of my Boyd's Bears blankets, I read what it said on this particular blanket. "Life is a Picnic." My initial thought after reading that was that life is not always a picnic. But as I've sat here and thought about it for a bit, I think that saying is true. Walk through a picnic with me. When I think of a picnic I think of three main things: blue skies, good food, and time to relax. Try to picture this picnic in your head. It's a beautiful sunny day and you've taken a blanket and spread it out underneath the shade tree and you pull out your food to have a nice little meal. You just want to kick back and spend some time with the person that you're with and just relax. Then you notice that ants are trying to eat your food and you spend time shooing them away, trying to position your food so they can't get to it. But they persist, and you find yourself not as relaxed because you're constantly fighting them. And then the wind picks up and out of the blue it starts thundering and next thing you know it's raining on your picnic.

Isn't that how life is? As we try to feed ourselves with godly things, there are always things that seem to pester us, even when we're trying to relax. And just when you think you can take a deep breath and exhale because life has settled down for you, another storm hits out of the blue. In Philippians 4:11-12, Paul tells us that he has learned to be content in whatever circumstances he found himself in and we can find that contentment, too. No, that doesn't mean we're going to enjoy those pesky ants and the different storms of life, but in the middle of those times, we can be satisfied that God is in control and up to something good in the midst of our troubles. And that's when we realize what verse 13 tells us. "I can do all things through Him who strengthens me." Here's to always making sure that we invite God to our picnics!

Lord, please help me learn to be content in whatever situation arises. With You by my side, I can do anything. Amen.

15...SEND ME

Good morning! My mind keeps going back to something my pastor said on Sunday. A survey that he saw on Google indicated that two-thirds of all the people on earth are not Christians. That means that Heaven is not their forever home and they have not received forgiveness of their sins by the Lord. Those numbers are just so hard to comprehend. What can we, as Believers, do about that incredible number?

The answer to that question can be found in the last two verses in the book of Matthew. God gives us these instructions. "Go therefore and make disciples of all the nations, baptizing them in the name of the Father and the Son and the Holy Spirit, teaching them to observe all that I commanded you; and lo, I am with you always, even to the end of the age." The Lord tells us that we are responsible for sharing the Good News of the Gospel. What we are not responsible for is their response. Salvation is an individual decision but those of us that have received this gift know that it is too great of a gift not to share with others. In the verses I referred to above, the baptism isn't what saves you. Only Jesus can save you. But the water baptism is an outward sign of our repentance and forgiveness of sins through the gift of Jesus Christ. Matthew 10:33-34 sums it up this way. "Everyone therefore who shall confess Me before men, I will also confess him before My Father who is in Heaven. But whoever shall deny Me before man, I will also deny him before My Father who is in Heaven."

Let's go back to that staggering two-thirds number. During the Christmas season, more people are thinking about Jesus because it's His birthday that we celebrate on December 25. This is a prime time for Christians to share the gift of salvation through Jesus Christ. My prayer is that we allow the Holy Spirit to guide us to those who need to hear about the best gift of our lives ... Jesus.

Lord, to those around me who don't know You, help me eagerly say, "Here I am Lord, send me!" Amen.

16...THE NORM

Good morning! As I looked at the weather forecast for the rest of the week, it was clear that we are now starting to experience some winter weather. It's predicted that the low temperatures will be in the 20's and the high temperatures only in the 30's and 40's. There's even a chance for some snow flurries. What cracks me up about that forecast is listening to people talk about it. We are in the month of December, after all, and these temperatures are what we are supposed to have this time of year in our part of the country. We've just been blessed with unusually warmer weather in the past weeks, so those warmer temperatures were the anomalies, not the temperatures forecasted for the rest of this week. Sometimes we just forget what the "normal" should be. This also happens in our Christian walk. Staying conscious of the Lord's presence should be our normal, but all too often we are like Jacob in Genesis 28:16 where he said, "Surely the Lord is in this place, and I did not know it."

Let me give you an example. I requested prayer for a couple of friends of mine. My friend had taken her husband to the ER the day before and they admitted him for observation. As she stayed with him in the hospital, she started feeling really bad. She was having a lot of pain in her right side and spiked a fever of 102.9. So, they sent her to the ER and the next morning she had her appendix removed. Should we be astonished that she was in the right place to get the care she needed at the right time? That was not an anomaly. The Lord is always with us and He orchestrates our life according to His plan, so there was no coincidence about my friend being at the hospital when her appendix decided it needed to come out. That was all God. That's just what He does. My prayer for us is that we strive to always be aware of the Lord's presence in our lives and to be thankful that He chooses being with us as the norm!

Jesus, thank You for always working things out for our best and for Your glory. And thank You for wanting to always be with us. Amen.

17...SUPERMOON

Good morning! Several days ago, we experienced what was known as a "supermoon." It is called a supermoon because it's substantially brighter than what a normal full moon would be. On the news, they said that this was the only supermoon that we will experience in the year 2017. Hope you had the chance to witness its beauty.

That moon got me thinking about the true Light of the World … Jesus. Until we asked Jesus to be our Lord and Savior, we were living in darkness. But once we accept the gift of salvation, we begin living in the Light, just like Colossians 1:13-14 tells us. "For He delivered us from the domain of darkness and transferred us to the kingdom of His beloved Son, in whom we have redemption, the forgiveness of sins."

Once we've been brought into the Light upon salvation, Ephesians 5:8-10 tells us that we are to walk as children of light and learn what is pleasing to the Lord. Others around us should be able to notice a change in our lives once we accept Jesus. We will still sin, but as we learn what pleases God, we should sin less, and others will notice that change. When people ask, "What's up with you?" since you are not doing or saying the things from the darkness you had been living in, you can tell them about the Savior that has brought you into the Light.

My prayer is that our lives will shine brighter than any supermoon and that others can see the Light of the Lord shine through us on a daily basis. Living in the Light of the Lord will help draw others to Him. Unlike the Supermoon, God's Light can be found every day of the year.

Lord, You truly are the Light of the world. Please guide my days so that Your light will shine bright through me. When darkness tries to close in, remind me that darkness and Light can't live together, and help me always choose You, the Light. Amen.

18...GOD'S AMAZING LOVE

Good morning! As I was reading in 1 John 4, I came across the title of verses 11-21 ... The Glories of Love. Many accurately call the Christmas season, the season of love because Love came down to earth through the birth of Jesus Christ on that first Christmas morning. 1 John 4:15-16 tells us that, "Whoever confesses that Jesus is the Son of God, God abides in him, and he in God. And we have come to know and have believed the love which God has for us. God is love, and the one who abides in love abides in God, and God abides in him."

Have you noticed how freely love flows this time of year? It flows to those we love and to total strangers. It flows to those who are experiencing tragedies and for those who are fighting illnesses. People also give more generously to charities this time of the year. I think we can answer the question of why love flows so freely around the holiday season quite simply ... people are focusing on God, regardless if they believe in Him or not. Have you ever noticed how people who say that they don't believe in God still celebrate Christmas? Since God is love, as they celebrate LOVE, they are also celebrating God, whether they understand that or not.

Since I don't know of anyone who doesn't believe in love, there's no better time than this season to help an unbeliever understand that God is love and He wants more than anything to share His love with them. So, during this Christmas season, pass on the gift that keeps on giving, for all eternity ... God's amazing love!

Lord, You are the reason why we can love. We look to You for the perfect example of love. Help us learn to pass on Your love to others every day of the year, not just during the Christmas season. You are the best gift we can share with anyone and that should be our goal. Holy Spirit, guide me to those who don't know yet about the Lord's amazing love. Amen.

19...A HELPING HAND

Good morning! I recently had a really nice guy come blow the leaves out of my gutters. As he put the ladder up to get on the roof, it reminded me of a story that took place with Alan several years ago.

I had just finished grocery shopping when Alan called me and asked if I was on my way home. I told him I was and asked him if he needed me to pick up anything before I left town. He said no but he'd let me pick something up for him once I got home. I didn't think too much of that response until I was coming down the lane to our house. And that's when I saw Alan. He was sitting on the roof, grinning from ear to ear. As I pulled into the driveway, I saw the reason he was sitting on the roof. The wind had blown the ladder down, so he was pretty much stuck on the roof until someone could put the ladder back up for him.

This incident reminds me of what we are told in Ecclesiastics 4:9–10. "Two are better than one because they have a good return for their labor. For if either of them falls, the one will lift up his companion. But woe to the one who falls when there is not another to lift him up." God never intended us to live this life by ourselves. It is much better to have a friend who can assist than trying to live life alone. Are you that kind of friend or family member to others? Do you look for ways to be helpful without being asked and then take the action necessary to fill that need? If you do, I can promise you that your life will be blessed. Here's to sharing God's love with others by offering a helping hand.

Lord, thank You for the reminder that we all need a helping hand from time to time. Please give us eyes to see and ears to hear what kind of helping hands others need. Then please let us be wise enough to extend the help they need. One day, we will need the help too, just like Alan. Amen.

20...OUR HELP

Good morning! Looking back at the story of Alan being stuck on the roof, I was reminded about some truths. First let me ask you a couple of questions. What would you have done if you had been left stranded on the roof? Would you have freaked out or would you have remained calm? Would you have tried to find a way to lower yourself to the ground without the ladder, which would have been dangerous? Knowing help was on the way, Alan was able to patiently wait until it arrived.

Do you ever have trouble waiting on the Lord? Even though we know it's in our best interest to wait on Him, we often get antsy as we wait, or at least I do. I want to be more like David in Psalm 121 and remember where my help comes from. Verses 1-2 explain this. "I will lift up my eyes to the mountains; from whence shall my help come? My help comes from the Lord, who made heaven and earth." David knew that the Creator of the mountains is the same Creator whom he had learned to trust for help.

We never know from minute to minute what life will bring us but there are a couple of truths we can stand on. If Jesus is our Lord and Savior, we know where to turn for help. From little things, like sending someone to give you a way off the roof, to big things like we read about through the life of David in the Bible. Once we've learned to trust the Lord in all things big and small, it's much easier to patiently wait for help to arrive, in whatever form God sends it. And while we trust and wait on the Lord to help us in our time of need, we can still keep our joy and enjoy life. So, here's to patiently and joyfully waiting for our ladder to arrive!

Lord, our help comes from You. Because we know You are always with, it is easier to wait for help when we need it. Just like with Alan, he joyfully waited for his help to arrive. Please remind me of this example when You see me impatiently waiting. It will bring a smile to my face, and more importantly, to my heart. Amen.

20

21...TEACH US

Good morning! As I was moving things around in my house, I came across a plaque in the shape of an apple. My sister gave me this plaque while I was still teaching. It has Psalm 27:11 printed on it. "Teach me your way, O Lord." During my teaching years, I kept it on my desk as a reminder to keep seeking God, especially when situations would arise that needed a fresh solution from Him.

As much as learning God's ways are important to our faith walk, I ran across another verse in Psalms this morning that will help us as we live out our days for Jesus. Psalm 139:23-24 says, "Search me, O God, and know my heart; try me and know my anxious thoughts; and see if there be any hurtful way in me, and lead me in the everlasting way."

Just knowing about God doesn't translate into a successful Christian life. As Christians, others look at us to see how we live out our faith. The verse in Psalm 139 reminds us that we need to continually ask God to search our hearts to see if there is anything blocking us from being all that He has created us to be. And once God shows us areas that we need to work on, we need to be faithful and let the Holy Spirit help us change our ways. Those that are watching how we live our lives will learn just as much, if not more, during our times of failure than those times when we have everything all together. So, here's to letting God teach us so we can in turn teach others through the example of how we live our lives for Him.

Heavenly Father, as we live our lives for You, we know we can't be those witnesses You have called us to be without Your constant help. As we study Your word and learn more about You, we pray that this would change the way we live. Thank You for Your patience as we learn to live out the life You have called us to. Amen.

22...TIMING

Good morning! I've been doing a lot of thinking lately about how the Lord wants us to wait on Him. There are situations in my life, like I'm sure there are in yours, that make me wonder how long the wait will be. As I wait, I was reminded about a story in Genesis dealing with Abraham and Sarah. Genesis 21:1-7 gives us that story of how God fulfilled the promise He had made to Abraham through Sarah by giving her a child in her later years. Abraham was 100 years old when his son Isaac was born. I don't know how long you've been waiting for God to handle whatever the situation is in your life, but chances are that Sarah and Abraham waited longer.

As I was reflecting on this story, I was reminded of the pain and heartache we can cause ourselves and others by not trusting and waiting on the Lord's perfect timing. Even though Sarah and Abraham caused themselves heartache when they took matters into their own hands with Hagar (Genesis 16), I wonder how Sarah and Abraham felt when Isaac was born. Was the birth of their son sweeter because they waited so long for him to be born, for God to fulfill His promise to Sarah? I think the process of waiting, even though we don't enjoy it much, makes God's answers that much sweeter. You know, there's not one story in the Bible that I've read where Jesus was in a rush to do anything. He didn't live a life of hustle and bustle like we all too often do. There are many reasons for why God has us wait but I wonder if one of the reasons is to make sure He has our full attention. Another reason might be so that there is no question as to Who brought the solution to our situation. With the story of Sarah and Abraham, there was no doubt, because of their age, that God brought them Isaac. Whatever you are waiting for God to handle in your life, let Sarah and Abraham's story reassure you that God will take care of everything … in His perfect timing.

Lord, help us wait for Your answers to our prayers. Help us not to take matters in our own hands instead of waiting for Your perfect timing. Amen.

23...SNOW DAYS

Good morning! To all my teacher friends, a big "woohoo" for your Christmas break is about to begin!! I received a text yesterday from a friend of mine that I used to teach with. She sent a picture she'd knew I'd enjoy. They received 6 inches of snow the night before so they were having a snow day!! Oh, how I loved snow days when I was teaching and everyone from my students to the superintendent knew it. The kids would yell down the hall when they came in from outside, "Mrs. Estes, it's snowing!!!" What they didn't know was that I'd already been doing the snow dance ... LOL

I was reflecting yesterday on why I loved snow days so much. I think the simplest answer is that it would give me an unplanned day. It would be a day that could just unfold naturally, without anything on my schedule. A day where I was able to hear God easier, without all the schedules and busyness of normal days interfering.

Psalm 46:10 tells us to just let go and let God be God, knowing He is in control, or that's how I paraphrase the verse. None of us know what we are going to encounter in our days, but God does. If you're like me, we try to schedule what will happen because we want control. But God wants us to let go of that control and have "snow days," where we give God our days and let Him do our scheduling.

Just as snow brings about peaceful tranquility, letting go and letting God be in control of every detail of our life brings about a peace that not even a snow day could compare to. Here's to not waiting for a snow day before we let God be God in our life. And if God wants to give us some snow, that would be the icing on our cake!!

Lord, please help us transfer the lessons we learn from having snow days to our everyday lives ... letting You schedule our days. Amen.

24...LIGHT AT THE END OF YOUR TUNNEL

Good morning! We live in such an instantaneous world. I think having all the technology that's available to us today helps make us want everything right now. When's the last time you marveled at the fact that you can send emails, text, or photos to someone hundreds of miles away in just moments? But here's a more telling question. When's the last time you got really aggravated when that same technology took a minute to work instead of merely seconds?

Patience is something I think everyone walking on the face of this earth struggles with. We want to get from A to Z at lightning speed. We often don't have the patience to get through the processes that are required in life. You know, like when a loved one dies, and you don't want to go through the grieving process. You just want to get to the other side of it, so the heartache will stop. Or when you're suffering with a physical ailment and you just want the healing to happen so that the pain will go away. And when there are broken relationships and you go through the "breaking up" process, there's pain there, too. God uses every ounce of our pain in life for His purpose and glory and our good. Not one single tear goes unnoticed by our Heavenly Father. When in pain, I go to a couple of verses for comfort. 1 Peter 5:10 says, "After you have suffered for a little while, the God of all grace, who called you to His eternal glory in Christ, will Himself perfect, confirm, strengthen and establish you." And 2 Corinthians 4:17 says, "For momentary, light affliction is producing for us an eternal weight of glory far beyond all comparison..." These verses comfort me because they remind me that the pain will end. These promises of God do not say that we don't have to go through the processes though. But based on these and many other promises, we know there is a light at the end of those painful tunnels. When our Light is Jesus Christ, we can endure the pain. Praying you can comfort someone in pain today with God's promises.

Lord, thank You that there is a light at the end of our tunnel and that the light is You. Amen.

25...SERVING OTHERS

Good morning! We are in the season of giving. Let's start today out with a few questions to ponder. When is the last time you gave a gift and expected nothing in return, not even a thank you? Or when is the last time you gave a gift anonymously? Do you give in order to receive the praise you'll get from others? Or do you give extravagantly so you'll out shine everyone else?

Matthew 6:3-4 tells us that "when you give alms, do not let your left hand know what your right hand is doing that your alms may be in secret; and your Father who sees in secret will repay you." Some of my greatest blessings have come from giving anonymously. I pray that those who have given to me in secret will experience great blessings, too. I think the question we really need to ask ourselves is, "What's our motivation for giving?" If we look to Jesus as our example when it comes to giving, our motivation should be all about serving others ... plain and simple, just serving others.

Some people go plum crazy with how much they spend on Christmas gifts. Some spend so much that they are paying for those gifts on credit cards all year long. I might look at things wrong, but I believe that our giving should just be a reminder of our love for those we give to instead of trying to "buy" their love by spending a fortune. Jesus showed us the best way to give...giving of ourselves. Money can't buy the feeling we get when we give of our time or talents to help others. During this holiday season, give a gift that only you can give by serving others. Let the gift of your time and attention be the one gift not on their list because they didn't know how such a gift would warm their heart. And you don't need a gift receipt either because this is a gift worth holding on to.

Lord, there is no one that can out give You. As we give, examine our hearts and bring to light any wrong motives we might have as we give to others. Thank You for giving us the perfect example for what it looks like to give from a pure heart. Amen.

25

26...FEASTS OF ALL FEASTS

Good morning! I've received gift cards to some of my favorite restaurants as Christmas gifts. And I have to admit, that excites me to no end!!!! I love eating out. Well, the truth is that I just love food in general. I had to ask myself after I used one of the gift cards this week whether it was ok to be this jazzed about food. But then I thought about all the references to food that we find in the Bible. There's the Lord's Supper, the feast with the story of the prodigal son, along with too many other feasts to count. I Googled to see how many verses mentioned food in the Bible and it said at least 112 times.

As I was reading some of those verses, I landed on one that seemed new to me. Matthew 22:2 says, "The kingdom of heaven may be compared to a king, who gave a wedding feast for his son." Wow, now that's a picture that I enjoyed putting in my head. One day, that mental picture will be a reality for all Believers. Can you imagine what that will be like???

But not everyone we currently know will be able to enjoy that feast. Only those that have accepted the gift of salvation will enter Heaven. The best Christmas gift that you could EVER give someone is Jesus. Helping someone understand that as sinners, which we all are, we are at odds with God. The only way we can be in His presence is to be holy. And since we can't fix that sin problem alone, God gave us a way through the shed blood of the perfect lamb, Jesus, to atone for our sins. Once you've accepted this in your heart and told God that you want this gift, you then become a child of God. As you enjoy your Christmas dinners, let the food remind you of what is waiting for every child of God. And then do what you can to share this Good News of Jesus so that everyone you know can enjoy the feast of all feasts waiting for Believers in Heaven.

Lord, how we await that feast with You in heaven. Nothing on earth can compare with what that glorious day will be like. Help us to tell others about this feast and what it takes to get an invitation. Amen.

27...THE GIFT OF JESUS

Good morning! During this time of year, little ones have made their list of things they want to receive from Santa. They wait with great anticipation for Christmas to arrive, so they can see if their wishes came true by the packages they open under the Christmas tree. There will be squeals of joy when they open that gift that they'd asked for. All will be well in their little world. Too bad we can't bottle that joy and spread it throughout the entire year.

I thought about this as I was reading in 1 John 4:13. "These things I have written to you who believe in the name of the Son of God, in order that you may know that you have eternal life." The most precious gift we could ever give our children is the gift of Jesus Christ. If we could help our kids understand who Jesus is and what He has done for us, Christmas would be much different for them. The gift of Jesus is eternal, unlike the Christmas gifts they receive from Santa. Wouldn't it be great if we spent as much time talking to our kids about the true reason for celebrating Christmas, which is Jesus, than we do making gift lists and having their pictures taken with Santa?

Leading our kids to the Lord would provide a gift for all eternity. They wouldn't need that bottle of joy I referred to earlier because they would carry with them a joy that surpasses all, knowing that they had been accepted by the Giver of joy Himself and that they'd belong to Him forever. That is my prayer for this Christmas season ... may true Joy reign forever!

Heavenly Father, help our heart's desire of wanting our kids and grandkids to grow up knowing You. There is no better time of the year to share with them all You are and what You mean to us. Thank you for helping us share our faith with them and thank You for the only gift that will last for all eternity ... Jesus. Amen.

28...LIGHTEN THE LOAD

Good morning! I stand in awe once again of how God takes care of everything He has created. Recently, I was playing outside with my dog, when I heard a flock of geese getting close. As they came over my house, I watched how they flew in an inverted V-shape. When the one in the front had flown in that position for awhile, he'd break off and go to the back of the flock where it's burden wasn't as great and another one would take the front position.

This reminded me of what God calls us to do. Galatians 6:2 tells us to, "Bear one another's burdens, and thus fulfill the law of Christ." When we have burdens too great to carry by ourselves, that's when as brothers and sisters in Christ, we are to come alongside and offer help. Each and every one of us will have our own load to carry, and God expects us to carry that load. But when life dishes out more than what we can handle alone, that's when we need the help of others.

Holidays are a really good time to help those whose burdens are many. It might be a single mom, who, even though she works a couple of jobs, can't afford to give her kids the Christmas that she'd like. It could be someone that has lost a loved one and the holidays just remind them of that void. Or it could be someone who is fighting a terminal illness wondering if this is their last Christmas. Whatever the need is, it doesn't take a lot to step in to help bear their burdens. As you pick up gifts for your loved ones, pick up a few extra and drop them off to a family in need. For those that have lost loved ones or are fighting a terminal illness, give them some of your time. Stopping by to just say hello and to give them a hug lets them know that they're not alone. So whatever God is calling you to do, I pray that you would be obedient. You might just be what they need to renew their hope.

Lord, thank You that Your Word shows us how we are to live this life. Help us lighten someone's load today. Amen.

29...KEEP TURNING THOSE PAGES

Good morning! Have you ever gotten so wrapped up in reading a great book that you've lost track of time? A good author will captivate you by bringing each character alive. As you read chapter after chapter, you can't read fast enough so you can turn the page to see what will happen next. I like the "happily ever after" endings to a book, but it doesn't always happen that way.

Our lives are often compared to a book. We go through chapter after chapter, daily turning the page to find out what will happen next. There will be twists and turns in the plot. We will experience things that we never thought would happen to us, both good and bad. We will take journeys that stretch us in all sorts of ways. We will gamble and take chances that we never knew we had the courage to do. We will experience great love, but also great loss. Sometimes we will feel like we are on a roller coaster, while other times we will be sailing on smooth waters. There will be times of prosperity, and seasons of need. Weeks will go by where we are confident of what will happen next and there will be times when we feel like we are flying by the seat of our pants, as the saying goes.

Even though we aren't sure about the events in our lives, God is. Jeremiah 29:11 tells us about God's plans for us. They are plans for "welfare and not for calamity to give you a future and a hope." One truth about our biographies is that our chapters are written by the world's best author, Jesus Christ. And the absolute best news is that if you're a Christian, you already know how the last chapter of your story will end. Our final destination is Heaven, where we will live happily ever after. Praising God for that truth this morning. Our beautiful and rich stories aren't finished yet, so keep turning those pages.

Lord, thank You for giving us the confidence that
our lives as Believers are securely in Your hands.
Thank You for the hope and future You give us.
Amen.

30...LONE RANGER

Good morning! Have you ever surprised yourself about how easy it is to open up to a complete stranger and once you left their company, you left having a new friend? Sometimes God makes it so easy to share our lives with others, when we let Him. Sure, it takes an element of trust to open up to others, but what a return we can get from that single act of trust.

Trust is a common thread that we find throughout scripture and in our Christian walk. A couple of my favorite verses deals with that issue of trust. Proverbs 3:5–6 says, "Trust in the Lord with all your heart, and do not lean on your own understanding. In all your ways acknowledge Him, and He will make your paths straight." Over the years, I've done a lot of trusting when it came to my physical heart. Over and over again, I laid it in God's hands through the skills He gave to different cardiologists and surgeons, and that trust continues today.

But God never intended me to be a "lone ranger" when it came to living with my day-to-day challenges. I thought that term was fitting as I recently opened up to a total stranger at the airport on my way to Texas. When we discovered we battled the same challenges, we started sharing things that had worked for each of us. That meeting was not by chance. God had His hand all over that encounter and because I took the risk to trust and open up, I was blessed. The next time you have the opportunity to talk to a total stranger, take it, instead of finding a way to avoid the conversation. Don't bury your head in a book or get on your phone. Put them down and you might just find yourself on the receiving end of a blessing that God wanted to give you!

Lord, You are so good to us. Thank you for giving us the courage to take risks in life. With You by our side, those risks turn into something beautiful. Thank You for the blessings that come as a result of opening up. Amen.

31...WELL DONE

Good morning! Life is all about choices. We literally make hundreds of choices each day. Some of the choices are routine, like choosing to brush our teeth daily. Some take just a little thought, like which path we want to use to drive to our destination. But then there are the choices that take work on our part.

Several people that I love dearly have chronic health conditions. Their conditions force them to constantly make the decision on how they will react to their situation. It warms my heart, and I know it does God's, too, when they carry on with life ... joyfully. They could be a total grouch and bark at everyone around them, but they have made the better decision ... to remain joyful.

In Titus 2:7-8, the apostle Paul was giving instructions on the duties of ministers. "In all things show yourself to be an example of good deeds, with purity in doctrine, dignified, sound in speech which is beyond reproach, in order that the opponent may be put to shame, having nothing bad to say about us." Since we are all called to be ministers of the Word, these verses apply to us, too.

Wouldn't it be great if we lived our lives with the joy that comes from the Lord? A life lived so others would not have anything bad to say about us. A life where all of our words and actions glorified God. A life spent lifting others up in prayer as we help carry their burdens. A life where we minister to others by giving of our time. A life where "self" took a back seat to others. A life where we lived each and every day with the sole purpose of glorifying God by serving others. Every day, may we make the joyful choices that would allow God to say, "Well done, my good and faithful servant."

Lord, how sweet it would be to live such a life that people would only have good things to say about us. I know that is the life we will live in heaven, but until You take us home, please give us the guidance so we can do just that here on earth. Amen.

32...RESTING

Good morning! Do you ever feel guilty about taking a nap? For years, I did. But that guilt stopped one day when I read 1 Corinthians 6:19-20. "Or do you not know that your body is a temple of the Holy Spirit who is in you, whom you have from God, and that you are not your own? For you have been bought with a price: therefore glorify God in your body." God gave us our bodies so we could use them to do the work He has laid out before us. He knows our physical limitations because He created us. If we need to rest in order to keep going, then a nap it is!

Just as sleep is important to our physical body, spiritually resting in the Lord is just as, if not more, important than physically resting. When we rest in the Lord, we are closing our minds off to everything else but Him. Although this time might seem unproductive, I promise you that the benefits of it far exceed anything else that we would do in the course of the day.

It's during this time that the Lord speaks to us and prepares us for what we'll experience throughout our day. It's time for us to just soak up all He wants to share with us. Sometimes He'll lead us to a particular Scripture that we need to read. Other times He will speak softly to us. Connecting this way with our Heavenly Father makes it easier to hear from the Holy Spirit. God wants us to be strong in mind, body, and soul. So, the next time you are feeling drained and need a nap, take it without any guilt, but also remember that God wants us to take time to sit quietly in His presence, too.

Heavenly Father, thank You for removing the guilt we often feel when we need to slow down and rest. This world encourages us to go, go, go but our bodies just can't take that pace. Help us see that resting in Your presence every day is crucial to our well-being. Amen.

33...REVEAL YOUR CHARACTER

Good morning! Something I do at the beginning of each new year is make a budget. It helps me see how I need to use the money God has so graciously provided me with. This budget is just a flexible plan that is subject to change as God instructs me differently, but it's a good place to start.

As I was reading in the New Testament, I noticed a notation that I had written after 1 Timothy 6:18-19. The note said, "When you see a dollar, be reminded that what you do with it reveals your character." Wow, now that will stop and make you think! We all need money to live, there's no getting around that. But God expects us to be good stewards with what He's given us. Since we are to be about Kingdom work, does our spending reflect that endeavor? Are we financially taking care of what's been entrusted to us, or are we living beyond our means?

We need to remember that those who have not yet come to faith in Jesus closely watch those who call themselves God's children. They look to see if their words and actions line up. With that being the case, as a Christian, being financially responsible is another way to be a good witness for the Lord. Living within our means shows others that God provides His children with what they need. As we begin a new calendar year, it would be good to prayerfully look over our finances to make sure they are pleasing to God, and make any changes God leads us to make.

Lord, help us find ways to bless others through the resources You have so graciously given us. Give us eyes to see the needs of others and show us how we can be an extension of Your love. Help us remember that those who don't yet call You Lord are watching Believers. Please help our words and actions line up. Help us be good stewards of what You have given us. Amen.

34...GOD CALLINGS

Good morning and Happy New Year! Now that we've begun a new year, do you have new year's resolutions? I usually just have a word or phrase that God has me focus on throughout the year. This year, my word is community. My goal is to discover how I can share Jesus more with others. The verses God gave me to focus on this year is Hebrews 10:23-25.

> *Let us hold fast the confession of our hope without wavering, for He who promised is faithful; and let us consider how to stimulate one another to love and good deeds, not forsaking our own assembly together, as is the habit of some, but encouraging one another; and all the more, as you see the day drawing near.*

I just finished reading the book, *The Turquoise Table* by Kristin Schell. It's a great book about reaching out to others for Christ's sake. If I had to sum up what I've taken away from this read, it would be that it doesn't take a huge production to reach others for Jesus. Quite the opposite is true. It's all about making ourselves available to others and just spending time with them. We love on them and then let God do the rest. In the book, Kristin talks about how she painted a picnic table turquoise and put it in her front yard and waited for people to come and sit at the table with her. It's a really cool book and well worth the time to read it. I remember asking myself, "Can it be this simple?" and after reading this book, I know the answer to that question is a resounding, "Yes!" We just have to make ourselves available to others.

What are your "God callings" for the new year? God might not be calling you to paint a picnic table turquoise and put it in your front yard, but He is calling you to something. My prayer for us as we begin a new year is that our focus would be on finding out what the Lord is calling us to do and then sharing Jesus with others as often as we can.

Lord, thank You for the beginning of another new year. We ask that You would guide and direct our steps as we start another fresh start to the next 365 days. May each step be taken for Your glory and good. Amen.

35...BEAUTIFUL PUZZLES

Good morning! A holiday tradition at my sister's house each year is putting a puzzle together as a family. The pieces are laid out on parchment paper on the table and then over the course of a few days, one piece at a time, the puzzle takes shape. One question I heard repeated this year was, "Why doesn't that fit here?" As I worked on this puzzle myself, I understood that question.

It reminds me a lot about how life is. Don't we wonder from time to time where our current puzzle piece will fit into our lives and whether the piece will be good for us? That question brings a verse to mind. Romans 8:28 reminds us that, "... God causes all things to work together for good to those who love God, to those who are called according to His purpose." The Lord is able to take all our pieces in life and create the perfect puzzle for us, but the caveat is that we must love Him. It's one of those "if-then" promises. "If" we love God, "then" He will work all the pieces of our life into a beautiful puzzle for us. So, how's your puzzle looking? I guess the better question is, does the promise of Romans 8:28 apply to you? If not, because you haven't asked Jesus to be your Lord and Savior yet, you can't expect all the pieces in your life to be arranged into that perfect puzzle. A personal relationship with God through Jesus is paramount to receive the blessings God wants to shower you with. You know, being in a garage doesn't necessarily mean you're a car, and likewise, being raised in a Christian home doesn't mean you're a Christian. It's a personal decision that only you can make. I can't think of any better way to start a new year than by making that decision for Christ or by helping someone else make that critical decision. So, here's to putting together beautiful puzzles!

Lord, what beautiful puzzles You can make out of our lives when we put our love and trust in You. For those who haven't accepted You as their Lord and Savior, show us what we can do to help them make the biggest decision of their life. Amen.

36...JUST WAITING

Good morning! One area in my Christian walk that I need to work on is the discipline of waiting. Are you a good and patient waiter?? Me, not so much. We don't like waiting in lines, or waiting in doctor's offices, or even waiting for a return phone call. I think waiting is so hard for us, or at least I know it's for me, because the world that we live in is so fast paced and things can be so immediate, especially with the internet. We don't want to wait on something that we think we could do quicker and without any waiting involved.

But that isn't what God has to say about waiting on Him. We are told over and over in scripture to wait on the Lord. Probably the verse that is used the most when it comes to waiting on the Lord is Isaiah 40:31. "Yet those who wait for the Lord will gain new strength; they will mount up with wings like eagles, they will run and not get tired, they will walk and not become weary." I love the promises that we see through this verse. God promises us strength, stamina, and endurance if we'd just wait on Him.

What are you waiting for as we start a new year? Maybe you're waiting for God to bring you a spouse, or maybe it's a job you're waiting for. For many, the wait deals with health issues. Whatever the wait is for you, we can stand on God's promises. Even though we dislike waiting, it's ALWAYS in our best interest to wait on the Lord, instead of being like a bull in a china shop and plowing through, getting totally ahead of God and forcing things to happen. When we don't wait on the Lord, we experience actually the opposite of what God promises. We get tired and stressed out instead of being strong and renewed. Knowing this, when I feel myself getting stressed out, I want to stop and check myself to make sure I'm not getting ahead of God. In my life, I want to follow God, and not the other way around. So, here's to the wisdom of waiting!!

Lord, please show us the importance of waiting for You. Speak to our hearts when we start to get ahead of You so we can take a step back and wait. Amen.

37...PASS ON GOD'S LOVE

Good morning! One of the things I love about how David wrote in the psalms is that he is so real with his thoughts and feelings. This morning I camped out in Psalm 27:13–14. "I would have despaired unless I had believed that I would see the goodness of the Lord in the land of the living. Wait for the Lord; be strong, and let your heart take courage; yes, wait for the Lord." We have all experienced times in our life when we have felt surrounded by troubles. It seems as though every time you turn around there is a new problem. It's as if the enemy is working overtime against us. The psalmist David understands. In these verses David shared that he would have greatly despaired if he didn't have the promises of God to stand on during those times.

Even the strongest of Believers can become weary and saddened by the people and events enclosing them. They can desperately want things to be different but when that doesn't happen their spirit can become overwhelmed. But what keeps them from sinking in a pit of despair are the promises of God. Just like David, we get our strength from the hope that we "would see the goodness of the Lord in the land of the living." Having the belief that God will cause things to change and work for good while we are still living here on earth gives us the hope we need to carry on. And the instructions David gives us to do while we are waiting helps keep us from crumbling under the pressure of the situation. "Wait for the Lord; be strong, and let your heart take courage; yes, wait for the Lord."

Do you know someone who is struggling with waiting to see God work in the land of the living? If so, stand with them and let them know that they are loved and not forgotten. I think one of the greatest pains we can experience in life comes with feeling that we're not loved. God loves us immeasurably and that's how we should love others, too.

Lord, help us pass on Your love to someone who needs that reminder today. Amen.

38...WHAT A FUTURE

Good morning! Have you written the numbers for the next year yet? (Example: 2019) Don't know about you, but I have to really focus on writing the correct year. As I paid bills, I had to go back and correct last year's numbers that I wrote on a couple of checks. There is so much more to a new year than having to write a new number on our checks. I love all the possibilities that a new year brings. I wonder if this year will bring improved health to the people I love. I wonder what God will do with my newest devotional that will be published. I wonder what new relationships He will bring to me this year. I wonder what ministry opportunities the Lord will give me and all the ways I'll be able to glorify Him. I wonder how He will move me in the area of community that He's given me to focus on this year. I wonder where He will have me live and what He will do with the farm that Alan and I had. And that list could go on and on.

Although I don't know what will come to pass during this next year, I am confident of a few things and I find them listed in Jeremiah 29:11. "'For I know the plans I have for you,' declares the Lord, 'plans for welfare and not for calamity to give you a future and a hope.'" God's plans for me will be for my good and they will give me a future and hope. And since all my hope is in Jesus, I say, "Bring on _____!" and all that Jesus has in store for me! My prayer for us this year is that we will be looking with great anticipation for whatever the Lord reveals to us. And for the plans He has designed especially for us, that we will be grateful for all of them because we can stand on the promise He gave us that everything will be worked out for our good.

Lord, we thank You for all that You will do in and through our lives in this new year. Help us to always remember Your promises. You gave them to us so that we could be encouraged that life is going as You have worked out for us. What a future we have with You in the middle of it! Amen.

39...JUST SPEAK

Good morning! Have you ever wondered what your name means? I was told at the airport that my name means "beautiful." I hope people can associate my name with inner beauty as it would be nice if others saw the Jesus that's within me. That is what I think would be beautiful.

Another precious name to me is the name of Jesus. The name of Jesus that was given to Him was so fitting since He came to save His people from their sins. John 3:17 says, "For God did not send the Son into the world to judge the world, but that the world should be saved through Him." A song that we sing at church has lyrics about the name of Jesus. "What a beautiful name it is, nothing compares to this, what a beautiful name it is, the name of Jesus." It is indeed a beautiful name! I don't know if my parents knew what my name meant when they named me Linda, but God knew exactly what Jesus' name meant when He told Mary and Joseph to name their baby Jesus...which means Savior.

We need to be as intentional as God was, when He named His Son Jesus, when we talk to others about our Lord and Savior, Jesus Christ. Maybe we could use the whole, "What does your name mean?" as a way to start talking to others about Jesus. The important thing for us to remember is that regardless of "how" we start talking to others about Jesus, that talking to others about Him is what we are called to do. You might feel awkward talking to others about Jesus at first, but I know from experience that God will take what we say, even in our awkwardness, and present it to the person we are talking to in whatever way that person needs hear it. He just wants us to be obedient and start talking. So, here's to speaking about the sweetest name I know … Jesus.

Lord, help us be obedient to our calling to tell others about You. Give us the courage we need to just start speaking, knowing You will do the rest. Amen.

40...GOD DOES BIG

Good morning! Growing up, I always heard that everything was bigger in Texas. In the part of Texas I was in recently, I'd have to agree with that statement. I was amazed at how big some of my favorite places were down there. One of my favorite chain stores was at least 50% larger in Texas and so was the restaurant I like to get soup from. It was amazing! Another thing I loved about Texas was how clean everything was, not just in stores and restaurants either. I saw street sweepers keeping the streets clean. It was just a pretty place.

Reflecting on Texas got me thinking about what was big in my life and what needed cleaning. I know I serve a big God, but do the things I do reflect that? I pray, but do I pray big? I believe, but do I believe big? I dream, but do I dream big? Hmmm...made me stop and think. Ephesians 3:20-21 says, "Now to Him who is able to do exceeding abundantly beyond all that we ask or think, according to the power that works within us, to Him be the glory in the church and in Christ Jesus to all generations forever and ever. Amen." That's my wake-up verse. It reminds me that God does BIG. He does BIGGER than I can even ask or think. So, do I pray, believe, and dream big? That's where my cleaning question comes in. I need to clean some things out of my mind to create space for the BIG that God has in store for me. There is so much that I store in my head that has no relevance to the Kingdom of God. There is no reason for me to keep it up there taking up space that could be used for a much better purpose. It requires me to let go of stuff ... pain, regret, guilt, unforgiveness, etc. In this next year, I'm stepping out of my normal and going big with God ... praying big, believing big and dreaming big! My prayer is that you would go big with God, too!!

Lord, as we start anew this year, help us to go BIG with You. We want everything You would like to give us. Help us get rid of the junk in our lives so we can make room for You to do the BIG in our lives. Amen.

41...GROWTH SPURTS

Good morning! While I was in Texas, I spent time with my three great nieces. They are 5, 3, and one-year old and are as sweet as can be. Don't kids that age seem to grow so fast? I believe the three-year old had a growth spurt while I was there.

Just as growth spurts are physically necessary, we have spiritual growth spurts, too. In my life, those periods of growth usually take place during or after times of trials and tribulations. They come when I realize that the only way I got through a particular situation was by totally depending on God. It's when I know He was the only reason I came out on the other side still in one piece. And every time that happens, my faith and trust in the Lord increases, aka ... a spiritual growth spurt. These periods of growth help us to know that the promises made in Psalm 34:17-18 are true. "The righteous cry and the Lord hears, and delivers them out of all their troubles. The Lord is near to the brokenhearted, and saves those who are crushed in spirit."

Haven't we all had those periods in our lives where we are just so broken-hearted that it's hard to get through the day? You know, when someone you thought would never hurt you, deeply causes you pain, or when a loved one dies, or when test results come back with what you never wanted to hear. Those are the days when I wonder, how can anyone get through this life without the constant help of the Lord? Because even with the Lord by our side, life can really be hard as it throws punches our way. Thankfully as believers, we can live knowing that we will never be separated from the Lord and that He keeps His promises, all of them. So next time life is pressing down on you, remember that growth spurts are necessary to increase our faith, but that God is always near during those times.

Lord, sometimes life is just hard to deal with. During those times when we are broken-hearted, thank You for sticking close to us and thank You for saving those that are crushed in spirit. We couldn't get through this life without You. Amen.

42...RUNNING HOME

Good morning! The actions of my dog often make me just shake my head as I wonder why he's doing what he's doing. I made him a really nice place to sleep on my front porch. I took a 55-gallon barrel and laid it on its side. Then I put half of a bale of hay in it and pushed the hay up on the sides of the barrel to form some good insulation. Then I placed a nice, soft doggy bed on top of the hay. It was a warm and cozy place for him to curl up and sleep through the night. But instead of doing that, he pulled the doggy bed out of the barrel onto the cold concrete porch. He pulled some of the hay out of the barrel too and then began pulling the stuffing out of the doggy bed. Oh my, what a mess! As I was thinking how foolish his behavior looked to me, I was reminded of the story of the prodigal son. As the story goes in Luke 15:11-32, the father had made very comfortable provisions for his son, but the son wanted to do things his own way, so he demanded his inheritance and off he went to do his own thing. The story ends with the son coming to his senses and returning home to his father after he had squandered all his inheritance and was starving.

I'm sure there are times when God just shakes His head and wonders why I'm doing things the hard and foolish way, too. He has given me all the provisions I need. He has also given me a clear understanding of what is right and what is wrong to protect me from the consequences of sin, but yet at times, I choose my own way instead. I was reminded of this when I heard the lyrics to the song, "Prodigal" by Sidewalk Prophets. The refrain of the song says, "*Wherever you are, whatever you did, it's a page in your book, but it isn't the end, your Father will meet you with arms open wide, this is where your heart belongs, come running like a prodigal.*" So as the lyrics say, you can always return to the Lord, whether it has been days, weeks, or even years since you were last with Him. Thankfully the Lord will always greet us with arms open wide.

Lord, thank You that You are always ready to receive us with Your love and forgiveness after we turn our hearts and lives back to You, just like the prodigal son. Amen.

43...CHOOSE JOY

Good morning! I'm pretty sure that most everyone would say that we are already experiencing an unusually cold winter. Even my family in Texas got snow flurries. My niece posted a video on Facebook of her three girls all bundled up running around their backyard enjoying their first experience with snow. The oldest one looked up and experienced what happens when you do that. You either get a snow flake in your mouth or your eyes. But once she realized that it melted, she went back to running around yelling, "snowwww, snowwww." It was too cute!!

This example shows that in life, even the unexpected can be joyful. So, when is the last time you found joy when God did the unexpected in your life? Maybe it was a good unexpected thing, like a snow day. That's easy to be joyful about. But what if the unexpected was something difficult, like a loved one passing away? I have several girlfriends, who like me, have experienced the unexpected death of their husbands. Obviously there is no joy in our loss but as we've decided, there is going to be joy in our new year. Each new year is a new beginning for all of us, and you, too.

You know, happiness is so fickle. It comes and goes depending on the circumstances, but joy is lasting. It's an intentional choice, regardless of your circumstances. Sorrow and suffering will pass but joy can remain forever. Our joy is found in the Lord...who He is, what He's done, and the promise of what He'll continue to do. As Nehemiah 8:10 says, "The joy of the Lord is my strength." Even when the unexpected isn't what you'd choose to happen, our joy in the Lord can be our strength, if we allow it to be. Here's to making the choice to be joyful, even when the unexpected is painful. Choose joy ... choose the Lord ... choose strength!

Lord, there are so many things in life that can drain our happiness but thank You that even in those times, You are our joy. Amen.

44...MAKING A WAY

Good morning! I was reading in Philippians and came across a verse that made me really stop and think. The apostle Paul was talking about his imprisonment because of his faith. He was encouraging others to stand strong in Christ. Philippians 2:27 says, "Only conduct yourself in a manner worthy of the gospel of Christ; so that whether I come and see you or remain absent, I may hear of you that you are standing firm in one spirit, with one mind striving together for the faith of the gospel..."

Paul suffered more for his faith than what we do. Sure, others might make fun of us because they don't know Jesus like we do, and they think we're a little crazy to believe in a God that can't be seen, but Paul was thrown in prison for his unyielding faith. Even with his suffering, Paul knew the gospel would make a way.

I was thinking about the different circumstances in life that initially bring us to the Lord. I heard a song on the radio that spoke to that point. The song is called, "The Gospel," and it's by Ryan Stevenson. The chorus of this song says,

"To the captive, it looks like freedom; to the orphan, it feels like home; to the skeptic it might sound crazy to believe in a God who loves, in a world where our hearts are breaking, and we're lost in the mess we've made, like a blinding light, in the dead of night, it's the Gospel, the Gospel that makes a way."

These words are so true. No matter what situation you find yourself in, it is the Gospel that will help you get through it. You don't have to struggle alone. Let others know your challenges so they can stand with you, just as Paul was encouraging others to do all those years ago. And together, through the help of the Gospel, Jesus will show us the way. So, here's to letting the Gospel make a way for you!

Heavenly Father, thank You that the Gospel does indeed make a way for us. Help us to be encouraged through Paul's life. Amen.

45...CHILDISH THINGS

Good morning! My dog cracks me up! The other night we had some freezing rain and sleet. We didn't get much accumulation, but enough to make streets and sidewalks slick. As I looked out to see how my dog was doing the next morning, this is what I saw. Cope was trying to walk up the icy sidewalk to the road. (My sidewalk has a slight incline.) Cope took a couple of steps up the sidewalk and then started sliding backwards. He jumped off onto the grass when he stopped sliding and then walked on the grass back to the porch and tried going up the sidewalk again. His results were the same. After he made several attempts, he returned to his house on the porch looking ever so defeated.

Don't we often use that same mindset? We lift our prayer requests up to the Lord and expect an answer to our prayer the way we see it's best. When we don't get that specific answer, we ask again, wondering why the Lord hasn't answered our prayer. We take a few steps forward as we wait and then, slide backwards, dejected that we haven't received our answer yet. And the whole time, God is saying, "Use the grass!"

I'm not sure if God chuckles as much at us as I did at Cope. 1 Corinthians 13:11 says, "When I was a child, I used to speak as a child, think as a child, reason as a child; when I became a man, I did away with childish things." God wants us to mature and grow in our faith by learning from past lessons He has taught us. God also wants us to look and listen for how He wants to answer our prayers. Not our way but His way should be our attitude. We too often though are like Cope. Doing the same old thing over and over, just like a child, and getting frustrated at the results. God doesn't want us to slip and slide through this life. He wants us to trust and listen to His direction. And many times, God wants us to walk on the grass.

Lord, help us to grow in You. Help us listen intently to Your directions. Thank You for being our Guide through life. Amen.

46...STEER CLEAR

Good morning! Driving on ice can be really sketchy, especially when it's black ice. I was amazed at all the pictures of weather related traffic accidents on the news. In hindsight, I'm sure those people wished they would have just stayed home. When I was learning to drive, my dad took me down to a department store parking lot to teach me how to steer out of a spin when you're on ice. I've always remembered that lesson, even though I haven't had to use it very much. The last time my car started spinning out of control was a couple of years before I retired from teaching. School was let out early because the snow and ice were coming down hard. I was driving slowly up a hill when I hit a patch of black ice. My car just started spinning around in circles. When I stopped, in the middle of the highway, I noticed that one of the ladies from school had witnessed it all. Boy was I glad my dad had taken time to teach me how to steer out of trouble. Without the lessons of the past, I could have ended up in a ditch or worse.

The same thing is true in our Christian life. I'm sure everyone can think of a time when something in their life was spinning out of control and the only way to get back to safety was by applying lessons we had been taught about God and the way He cares for us. In John 16:33, Jesus tells us that we should expect to have trouble in this life but that we can have peace in spite of these trials because He has "overcome this world." If you're not sure how to use those things that God has set up for us to steer out of problems, hook up with a seasoned Christian and let them help you get control again. There are answers to our problems in the Bible, but sometimes we just need a little help finding them. Here's to knowing when to keep your foot off the brake as you steer into the problem and letting God bring you safely back home.

Lord, thank you for giving us directions to keep us out of trouble. But when we find ourselves in difficulties, remind us that You are all we need to steer things in the right direction again. Amen.

47...OUR TREASURES

Good morning! Where are you storing your treasures? I've been talking to God a lot lately about my priorities. I want to make sure they are lining up with His plans for my life. This morning I was led to read a parable in Luke. Luke 12:16-21 tells the story of a rich man that had very fertile land, which should be a blessing. But, the parable continues with the man reasoning with himself (How often do we do that??). He decided to tear down his barns and build bigger barns, so he could store up grains and goods for many years to come, allowing him then to take it easy. "Eat, drink and be merry," was his plan. But God said to Him, "You fool! This very night your soul is required of you; and now who will own what you have prepared?" The lesson of this parable is that the man who lays up treasure for himself, is not rich towards God. And a man that is not rich toward God hasn't stored up treasures in Heaven.

The things of this world are so temporary. Watch the news and you will see how fires and natural disasters destroy people's possessions on a regular basis. And then what are we left with? Throughout Scripture, we are told to lay up our treasures for eternity, not for here on earth. In order to do that, we must be concerned with God's priorities for our lives. Our lives should be about serving others, instead of serving ourselves. By serving God this way, we will be storing up our treasures in heaven where they can't ever be destroyed, unlike earthly treasures that could be gone in a flash.

So back to the initial question I asked. Where are you storing your treasures? Matthew 6:21 gives us the answer. "...for where your treasure is, there will your heart be also." My prayer is that our hearts will be with God. And if our hearts are with God, then we will be serving others, not self.

Heavenly Father, what would You like for me to do today? Show me ways in which I can serve others. Please give me eyes to see and ears to hear so I don't miss any opportunities You have for me. Amen.

48...THE FULLNESS OF GOD

Good morning! As I sit here looking at a canvas my girlfriend painted of Alan and I overlooking the Pacific Ocean on our trip to California many years ago, a few things are running through my head. The first thought was remembering how vast we thought the ocean was. It seemed to go on forever. It was cool how it had so many different shades of blue running throughout it and how white the waves were that crashed over the rocks. I remember us talking about how amazing it was that as powerful as the ocean was, that God's power was greater. His power caused the water to stop at the shore. Have you ever thought about that???

As vast as the ocean is, I'm reminded of something much greater...God's love for us. The Apostle Paul talked about this in the third chapter of Ephesians. In verse 18, Paul's hope for all believers is that we would be able to comprehend what the length and width, height and depth of God's love is for us. In verse 19, we find the rest of Paul's hope for us. "...and to know the love of Christ which surpasses knowledge, that you may be filled up to all the fullness of God."

I really believe we just can't fully comprehend the vastness of God's love for us. It's greater than anything we could fathom. I think our understanding is comparable to just a few drops of water versus the entire ocean. For me, every day I live with the Lord as my guide, I understand the love He has for me a little bit more. And the benefit of that clarity is that I'm then able to pass that love of His on to others. So, the next time you're not feeling loved, think about the vastness of the ocean and let it remind you that God loves you way more than that!!

God, the vastness of Your love for us is truly hard to comprehend. One day we will fully understand it but for now, help me see more and understand more of that love You have for us each and every day. Amen

49...ALWAYS WAIT

Good morning and yikes! I just read a story in the Old Testament about what happens when we don't wait on the Lord and instead take matters into our own hands. This story is found in 1 Samuel 13:1-14. As the story goes, Saul had been ruling for thirty-two years over Israel. He was gathering his men to fight a battle and was supposed to wait for Samuel to arrive to offer the burnt offering to the Lord before continuing. But as Saul saw his people scattering and the Philistines gathering their men for battle, he became fearful and offered the burnt offering himself to unite his people and prepare for war, instead of waiting for Samuel. The problem with this was that Saul was not appointed to offer this offering to the Lord, Samuel was. When Samuel arrived, he confronted Saul about why he didn't wait. Instead of owning his sin, Saul tried to justify his actions. Verses 13 and 14 conclude this story. "And Samuel said to Saul, 'You have acted foolishly; you have not kept the commandment of the Lord your God, which He commanded you, for now the Lord would have established your kingdom over Israel forever. But now your kingdom shall not endure. The Lord has sought out for Himself a man after His own heart, and the Lord has appointed him as ruler over His people, because you have not kept what the Lord commanded you.'"

Not waiting on the Lord and taking things into his own hands cost Saul his reign over Israel. Did you catch the word in those verses that show us just how colossal his mistake was? Samuel told Saul that the Lord would have established his kingdom over Israel FOREVER!! If only Saul would have waited...So what are you waiting on the Lord for? Have you been waiting awhile? Are you about ready to pull a "Saul move" because your situation is getting a bit too scary for you? Let this story serve as a warning. Waiting on the Lord is ALWAYS the right choice. Whatever your battle is, wait on the Lord and trust Him to fight it for you.

Lord, please help me to be obedient to Your instructions and not to get ahead of You and take things into my own hands. Amen.

50...SHARE THE TRUTH

Good morning! This morning my heart is still heavy. Yesterday there was another school shooting. This time in Benton, Kentucky. The location is different, but the results are the same. Lives will forever be changed from another senseless act. My heart breaks for all involved. In the world we live in today, there are so many voices that our kids hear. Sadly, many of the voices are coming from the enemy. As Believers of the God who created all mankind, we have a job to do and we need to be very intentional about doing it. We need the positive voices that speak of love, forgiveness, and hope to ring louder than the voices coming from the evil one. When we see tragedies like this school shooting, our hearts should be stirred and our desires for all to come to Jesus should be paramount in our lives.

We don't know what was happening in the life of this shooter that drove him to shoot his classmates. But what I do know is that we serve a good God. A God that is greater than any tragedy. A God that can take broken and make it whole again. A God that takes the seemingly impossible and makes it possible. A God that understands evil and offers good in its place.

The crucial question that needs to be asked this morning is, "What are you doing to pass on your faith in the Lord Jesus Christ?" Do the people in your immediate world even know you are a Believer? Does your life show others the hope you have through Jesus? Are you a reflection of a good, good God? We need to be God's workers here on earth to help bring people to the truth. My prayer for all of us is found in Philemon 1:6. "...and I pray that the sharing of your faith may become effective for the full knowledge of every good thing that is in us for the sake of Christ."

Lord, there is so much evil in our world, but that was also true when You walked the face of this earth. Help us pass on to others the hope only found in You. Amen.

51...DIFFERENT PATHS

Good morning! From my house, I can literally take half a dozen different paths to get to the closest city. Each path varies in length and ease but they all end up at the same destination. Have you ever had someone get aggravated with you because you drove a different way to get somewhere? They thought their way was the best and therefore, the only way to go. Many Believers are guilty of this, spiritually speaking, thinking they have the perfect route. You see, we are all traveling on a different path in life, even though our final destination of Heaven is the same. God directs each believer down the road He has laid out for them individually. We can have similar experiences, but they won't be exactly the same. Since I am a widow, I can relate with other widows, but I can't know exactly what they are going through, because their situations are different.

What are we to do since all our situations in life are different? 2 Corinthians 1:3-4 answers that question for us. "Blessed be the God and Father of our Lord Jesus Christ, the Father of mercies and God of all comfort; who comforts us in all our afflictions so that we may be able to comfort those who are in any affliction with the comfort with which we ourselves are comforted by God." Even though our lives are not exactly the same, we receive some of the same things from God. I might not have been married to Alan for 50 years but I know how God has comforted me through my loneliness. That's the thing I can relate to with other widows.

Even though our destination, Heaven, is the same for all Believers, our roads are different. The only thing that has to be common with all Believers is that we have accepted Jesus as our Lord and Savior. From that part of our journey forward, we all travel a different road designed for us by God.

Lord, help us be supportive of the roads You have set out for others to travel. Thank You that as Believers, we all end up in heaven with You for all eternity. Amen.

52...CONSTANT REMINDER

Good morning! Nothing seems to stop us in our tracks as fast as a diagnosis of cancer, or as one of my girlfriends call it, stupid cancer. Her assessment is 100% right. With this stupid cancer comes changes and uncertainty. Treatments for it can include surgery, chemotherapy, or radiation...all things that make us cringe. Getting better usually means a period of unpleasant treatment. There is a lot of unknown when it comes to this stupid thing.

But there is also a lot of certainty to consider. Hebrews 13:8 tells us that "Jesus Christ is the same yesterday and today, yes and forever." So, what does that mean? It means that God is much greater than any stupid cancer. He uses all sorts of ways to heal us, mostly from the inside out. He is concerned about every minute of your cancer journey. He is good about putting people in your life so that they can be His hands and feet of compassion. It means that He will never leave or forsake you. He is with you every step of the way. It means that He understands your pain and fear of this unknown. He knows your every thought and sees your every tear. He will provide for your needs, just as He has done in the past. And it also means that you can still experience peace and joy as you go through this cancer journey. No, not happiness that you have cancer. That would be crazy, but joy that comes from knowing that God's promises are still as true today as they were in the past. Joy that comes from knowing that He wants to continually hold your hand. Joy that comes from knowing that He has gone before you and all you have to do is take one step at a time. Joy that comes from not having to look down the road because you know God has already done that for you. And the joy that comes from knowing that you are not alone. Let me repeat that ... You are NOT alone! God will never leave your side.

Lord, for all those that are being impacted by cancer, we ask that You show Yourself BIG in their lives. Help us to constantly remind them that You have them in Your loving hands. Amen.

53...HE USES IT ALL

Good morning! When you think about your current life, do you wish you were in a different season of life? Over the last few days, I have really, really, really been missing Alan. Grief is one of those things where it just pops up for no apparent reason. This is a situation I can't change. But as I was reminded yesterday, I am in this season and God expects me to take the next step each day. God doesn't want me to dwell about yesterday and all the "what-if's" that could have happened, like what life would be like if Alan was still here. And God doesn't want me to worry myself about tomorrow. He wants me to just live in today, which is good because that's exactly where God is...in the here and now.

Because we are not God, we have no way of knowing what things He is using from our lives today to help orchestrate the events of the future. God uses everything in our lives, even the stuff we think is meaningless, like our day to day chores. God even gives meaning to those things. 1 Samuel 16 tells the story of David being anointed as king over Israel. The Lord told Samuel to go to Jesse's place and He would anoint the one He had chosen. Samuel was sure that the first son of Jesse that he saw would be the one that the Lord would designate. But it didn't turn out to be the case, nor did he choose any one of the rest of the boys that were there. When Samuel asked Jessie if this was all of his children, Samuel told him that his youngest was tending sheep. Samuel told Jessie to send for him. Verse 12 tells what happens next. "So he sent and brought him in. Now he was ruddy, with beautiful eyes and a handsome appearance. And the Lord said, 'Arise, anoint him; for this is he.'" There David was, taking the next step, doing the day-to-day task of tending the sheep, not knowing he was about to be anointed the King of Israel, and then God called him.

Lord, thank you that You will use whatever season of life we're in to fulfill Your purpose for us, just like You did with Jesse's son, David. Help us to say "yes" when You call on us. Amen

54...MASTERPIECES

Good morning! One of my indoor hobbies is scrapbooking. Lately, I've been making a lot of cards. I love how each card starts out with the same blank card and then piece by piece I start transforming it into something very unique. The more cards I make, the better the design becomes because I build on the beauty of the previous designs.

My inspiration for the design of these cards comes from lots of different things. I think my favorite card that I've recently made was inspired by a mug that my sister gave me. I was enjoying some hot chocolate and as I put the mug on the table, the light bulb turned on as I realized that the pattern on the mug would make a cute card. And indeed it did!

You know, our Christian life is a lot like scrapbooking. God takes us all while we were still sinners (the blank card) and little by little, piece by piece, He changes us. I like how 2 Corinthians says it. "But we all, with unveiled face beholding as in a mirror the glory of the Lord, are being transformed into the same image from glory to glory, just as from the Lord, the Spirit." Day by day, as we focus on the Lord, we will become more like Him. As we read Scripture and sit quietly in His presence, pray, and spend time with other Believers, we will soak up the characteristics of the Lord and He will continue to change us to be more and more like Him.

Just like each of the cards that I make are unique, we are all one-of-a-kind masterpieces of the Lord. He has designed us all to be different. But in each of us, there is a void in our life that can't be filled by anyone or anything other than the Lord. Once we accept Jesus as our Lord and Savior and that void gets filled, then God can build on that solid foundation and begin to transform us day by day.

Heavenly Father, thank You for taking each of us and turning us into masterpieces made in Your image. Amen.

55...TOSS OUT WORRY

Good morning! I love the sunny day we had here yesterday. The sunshine sure picked up people's spirits. I've been thinking a lot about people's spirits lately. My pastor said something at church on Sunday that has been replaying over and over in my head. In life, we are going to have worries or concerns. That's just normal. But we need to choose to not let those worries and concerns "have us." It's kind of crazy, but I know we all do it. Something happens that causes us concern and then we start rolling it over and over in our head. As it rolls, we add to the worry things that could happen, making the concern even worse. And before we know it, that concern takes on a life all of its own and that's when the worry "has us."

There are so many problems that come about when worry "has us". First of all, it consumes our thoughts, and then we don't have room for any positive thoughts to come through. When that happens, we push God out as well, which is crazy because He is the One who can take care of our concern. And then when we add our emotions into that mix, it's a cocktail for disaster. I don't know about you, but when I've done that, it seems to take too long for me to figure out what's happening. So, I'm starting to put reminders around my house to help me identify quicker when things become worrisome. Reminders like Psalm 121:8, "The Lord will guard your going out and your coming in from this time forth and forever." God watches over believers all the time, in every circumstance and forever. Knowing that promise, what do we have to worry about? Really, what would it be??? Like so many other things, worrying is a choice we make. Unfortunately, that choice will get us nowhere... nowhere good anyway. The next time you feel yourself getting tied up in knots over worry, make the choice to kick worry out, and focus on the God that has your back. Your spirits will be lifted as the Son will shine through you!!

Lord, help us to toss our worry out the window and turn our thoughts to You, the One who can handle our concerns. Amen.

56...LEAPING FOR JOY

Good morning! Have you ever noticed that with different translations of the Bible a word or two might be different in a verse but that using that different word gives you a different mental picture? Here's an example. The main difference between the NASB and the NIV translations of Psalm 28:7 is one phrase. The NIV reads, "The Lord is my strength and my shield; my heart trusts in Him, and He helps me. My heart leaps for joy, and with my song I praise Him." Instead of "my heart leaps for joy," the NASB version says, "therefore my heart exults." Both translations mean the same but leaping for joy rang true to me because as I was growing up, my dad called me "leaper" because I was forever doing the happy dance about something. The difference between then and now is the "why" behind my leaping.

As a child, I would leap for joy when I was happy about something. You know, like when we'd win a softball game or a tennis match, when I knew we would be having one of my favorite meals or when I knew I'd get to visit my grandma. All things that made me very happy. But now I leap for joy over things of the Lord. Things like answered prayers for when a friend gets a clear cancer scan, or when God once again provides for my needs. The difference between when I was a child and now is that as a child I focused on what made me happy. But those happy things were short lived. Now as an adult who has given her life to Jesus, my focus is on what makes Him happy, and those things carry a long-term effect. I was a happy, little giggle box of a girl growing up and it didn't take much for me to do the Happy Dance but I didn't have a grasp as to where that bubbling joy came from. Thankfully as an adult, I know my joy comes from the Lord and I still leap for joy over what God is doing in my life and in the lives of those I love. But now I know whom to give thanks to as my source of that joy...God, and God alone.

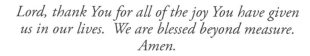

Lord, thank You for all of the joy You have given
us in our lives. We are blessed beyond measure.
Amen.

57...OUR REFUGE

Good morning! When I was growing up, we had the coolest treehouse. It was built on the strong branches of a huge weeping willow tree in our backyard. The tree's thick canopy allowed us to be in the treehouse even if it was raining and we'd still stay dry. It was a great place to just hide out because no one could see if you were in there or not.

As I was reminiscing about these childhood memories, I began thinking about where I take refuge as an adult. Where do I go to just rest and feel safe? When Alan was here, he always told me that no matter how crazy the outside world was, if we both could just get back to our piece of heaven that we called home, together the three of us could weather any storm. The three of us being God, Alan and me. He was right about that.

So where do I go now to feel safe and secure, with Alan being in heaven? The same place we went as a couple...to God. Psalm 18:30 says, "As for God, His way is blameless; the word of the Lord is tried; He is a shield to all who take refuge in Him." You see, it wasn't our home that brought us that safe and secure feeling. It was being in the arms of God. Resting in the promises of God brought us that peace we needed. It wasn't the slice of Heaven where we lived together that was our refuge. It was being together under the Lord's canopy. Even though Alan is gone, I can still enjoy that same refuge in the Lord. We all can. I could sell my home and acreage and move into a new place and carry that peace with me because it's not about the home, it's about the heart. So where does your heart take refuge? I know of only one place where we can find security to weather any storm that rains in our lives and that is in the Lord. He wants to put a canopy of protection over you. Under that roof, with the Lord by your side, together you can handle anything in life...the good, the bad, and even the ugly.

Lord, thank You for being the refuge we need to handle the storms in life. We are always safe in Your arms. Amen.

58...JUST FOR GOD

Good morning! I have a sweet friend who is an amazing painter. It's truly a gift from God because she has never had any formal training. The picture my friend painted for me was of my oldest granddaughter riding on one of our horses, Bandit. My granddaughter was singing to Bandit as she rode him up and down the road. Hard telling how many trips they had taken, but Bandit was getting tired. He had his head down as he slowly walked. But he kept on walking because that is what we asked of him.

I was thinking about how Bandit knew he had a job to do and he did it well. We asked and he complied. Colossians 3:23 tells us to do the same thing. "Whatever you do, do your work heartily, as for the Lord rather than man." I'm sure we've all heard the phrase, "be the best you can be." That's basically what we are being told to do in that verse in Colossians. Can you imagine what our world would be like if everyone did everything they did during the course of our days as though they were doing it for God? If we gave our best to our family, our church, our employer or employees, our neighbors, and our community, oh what a difference we'd see!!

Verse 24 in Colossians 3 says, "knowing that from the Lord you will receive the reward of the inheritance. It is the Lord Christ whom you serve." If only we'd take that verse to heart, we'd do everything we did with the motivation of just wanting to please God. We'd seek His approval, not the approval of those around us. That would be so freeing...to everyone. My prayer for us is that we'd all live with the purpose of pleasing God and that we'd look only for His approval. In doing this, we'd see such a positive change in all of our lives.

Lord, if we could only get this one command right, doing all we do just for You, what a difference we'd see in our lives and in this world. Please help us to only seek Your approval for what we do with our days. Amen.

59...IT'S JUST THAT EASY

Good morning! An irony that keeps running through my head is that we, as believers, trust God with our eternity but have trouble trusting Him with our day-to-day circumstances. Isn't that crazy?? If we can trust Him for our eternal security, we can also trust Him for our earthly needs. So, the question we really need to answer is "why don't we trust Him?"

I think for lots of us, we can find the answer to that question by looking at a couple of things that keep us from totally trusting the Lord. The first is our control issues. Here on earth, we think that we should be able to control what happens in our life. Lack of control often wigs us out. We often feel like God needs our help in taking care of what is happening in our lives, which of course is the furthest thing from the truth. Sure, God often lets us take a role, but He doesn't need us to accomplish His plan. The second thing that hinders us is the feeling of weakness. It's often hard to just accept our circumstances. We forget that God has control over everything and that He wants to guide us through our days.

So, what is our part in all of this? We are to trust in the Lord, rely on His strength, and rest in His peace. It sounds too simple, doesn't it? It's just like our salvation sounded too simple, too, when all we have to do is accept the gift of salvation God offers us through the shed blood of His Son, Jesus Christ. It sounds way too easy, but it is just that simple. Psalm 29:11 gives us the promise we need to hold on to as we live out our life here. "The Lord will give strength to His people; the Lord will bless His people with peace." My prayer for us today is that we would finally stop making things so difficult and instead just hold tight to the Lord's right hand as we take this day one step at a time, being willing to go wherever He leads us.

Lord, help us to trust in You as we know You are in control of everything. Help us deal with our control issues and understand that when we are weak, You are strong. Amen.

60...ALWAYS IN HIS THOUGHTS

Good morning! Have you ever had one of those days where everything seemed to be a challenge? The problems weren't big in themselves, just frustrating and one mishap led to another. You know, when getting out of the door in the morning took twice as long as it should have and by the time you were able to leave, you felt like going back to bed but you couldn't because you just realized you locked the keys to your house inside your home. And the crazy morning continues as everyone "thinks" they need something from you and you just wanted five minutes to yourself. A day when you just wanted to run a quick errand, but it takes up your entire lunch and you didn't get to eat anything, leaving you "hungry." And just when you've had enough of that day, someone sends you a text just to say hi and to see how you're doing. That's it, no strings attached, no secret agenda to get something from you, just a friendly hello. Then a smile comes over your face to replace the tense look you were just sporting. And you say to yourself, "Wow, that was nice. I needed that!"

It's so nice to be thought of by others, but what's nicer is that God Himself has us constantly on His mind. He is thinking about us every minute of every day. Psalm 139:17-18 says it like this,

> *How precious also are Thy thoughts to me, O God! How vast is the sum of them! If I should count them, they would outnumber the sand. When I awake, I am still with Thee.*

It's mind-boggling to me that the Creator of Heaven and Earth is always thinking about me. But the news gets even better than that because He is a God of action. He is orchestrating the events of our lives, always working to bring good out of our circumstances. So the next time the Holy Spirit brings someone to your mind, take the time to let them know you're thinking about them. And it would also be a great opportunity to remind them that God NEVER stops thinking about them. Now that's a piece of information that will definitely brighten their day.

> *Lord, thank You that we are always in Your thoughts. Help us to keep You first and foremost in our thoughts as well. Amen.*

61...BLANKET OF PEACE

Good morning! As I was asking the Lord to bless each of you this morning, I was reminded that there are some really huge needs out there that only God can take care of. If I just focused on everyone's needs, they could really weigh me down. Last night I went to the funeral home for the visitation of a friend's husband. That's not a place I like to be, especially with it being the same funeral home that I used for Alan. As I was waiting in line to offer my condolences, my heart started breaking all over again for her because I know what she will be experiencing without her husband. The loss is hard. I began praying for the one thing I knew she needed ... God's peace. Recalling and praying Scriptures calmed my heart too.

And the peace of God, which surpasses all comprehension, will guard your hearts and your minds in Christ Jesus. -- Philippians 4:7

The Lord will give strength to His people; the Lord will bless His people with peace. -- Psalm 29:11

Now may the Lord of peace Himself continually grant you peace in every circumstance. The Lord be with you all! -- 2 Thessalonians 3:16

No matter what circumstances you are experiencing, the Lord is wanting to replace your anxiety, brokenness, fear, anger, loss, depression, or whatever you're feeling with His peace. And just like what I prayed for my girlfriend last night at the funeral home, I pray that you feel the Lord wrapping you up in His blanket of peace, allowing the weight of your circumstances to melt away when you hand it over to the Lord. The problem will still be there, but God will be carrying it for you.

Lord, help us to take in a long, deep breath and slowly exhale knowing You have us and whatever we are facing in Your tender, loving care. Amen.

61

62...MAKING LEMONADE

Good morning! I recently got rid of an old entertainment center. As the guys tried to carry it out my front door and up the sidewalk to the truck, it broke into several pieces. So, we went to Plan B. I took the door off the entertainment center and we trashed the rest.

Norman Vincent Peale's quote is one people recite often to those facing challenges. "When life hands you a lemon, make lemonade." The glass door from the entertainment center now rests against a wall in my living room with four reminders of how I want to live when life gives me lemons. The vinyl letters I put on the glass door say, "JOY unspeakable, FAITH unsinkable, LOVE unstoppable, ANYTHING is possible." 1 Peter 1:8 tells us that we can "greatly rejoice with joy inexpressible..." I want to have unsinkable faith, just like those saints we read about in the Bible. I'm confident in love unstoppable because Romans 8:38-39 tells us that "nothing can separate us from God's love." And I know all things are possible with God because Jesus spoke those exact words in Matthew 19:26. "With people this is impossible, but with God all things are possible."

The apostle Paul talks about the persecutions he endured in 2 Timothy. In Chapter 3 verse 11 he says this about them: "...and out of them all, the Lord rescued me!" Paul kept his focus on the Lord and did Kingdom work no matter where he was, even when he was in prison. So when we face uncertainties in life, we can either give up, or be like Paul and "God-up." From my own experiences, the second option is always the best. God hasn't given up on us and we definitely don't need to give up on Him. I know waiting patiently is difficult but it's something we need to do because God's timing in the end is always perfect. As we wait on the Lord, I think a glass of lemonade is in order.

Lord, we know that not everything goes smoothly in life and so help us to find ways to make lemonade out of the tough times. With You, it is always possible. Amen.

63...AMAZING LOVE

Good morning! This weekend I watched the opening ceremony of the Winter Olympics. As I watched the Parade of Nations, many things came to mind. The first thing I noticed was how many of the athletes had their cell phones with them and were taking selfies and recording their own videos. When they put their cell phone on a selfie stick, all the athletes looked like they could be Americans. The second thing I noticed was that there was universal language present … love. It showed itself through all the athlete's smiles that were representing the 92 countries and territories. But the third thing I noticed is where I want to wave the flag for a minute. Some of the countries that were represented only had one athlete competing in these winter games. I was struck by the fact that their countries supported them even though they were the lone athlete. The same fanfare and recognition was given to them as the countries that had hundreds of athletes participating.

God is the same way. If you or I had been the only sinner on earth, because of His great love for us, He would still have sent His Son, Jesus, to die for our sins. Why would He do that? 2 Peter 3:8-9 gives us that answer. "But do not let this one fact escape your notice, beloved, that with the Lord one day is as a thousand years, and a thousand years as one day. The Lord is not slow about His promise, as some count slowness, but is patient toward you, not wishing for any to perish but for all to come to repentance." Now that is real love! God wants all of us to have time to accept Him as their Lord and Savior. My question for us today is what flag are we waving in our daily lives? Figuratively speaking, are we proudly displaying the Christian flag by celebrating all that God is, all that He has done, and all that He promises to do in the future? Are we sharing the Good News of Jesus Christ to this hurting world? As cool as it was for the athletes of all those countries to proudly wave their country's flag, it's much better to wave the flag of Jesus Christ and to pass on the universal language of His love!

Thank You, Lord for the amazing way You love us! Amen.

64...FREEDOM TO WORSHIP GOD

Good morning! You know, freedom is something I think we take for granted, especially the freedom we have to openly worship God in this country. There are so many places in this world in which worship must happen secretly for fear of retribution. Yet here in America, it seems like there is a church on every corner. What do we do then with that freedom we have to worship God openly? Do you share your faith with others or do you keep it to yourself? Matthew 5:14-16 says,

> You are the light of the world. A city set on a hill cannot be hidden; nor does anyone light a lamp and put it under a basket, but on the lampstand, and it gives light to all who are in the house. Let your light shine before men in such a way that they may see your good works, and glorify your Father who is in heaven.

Those verses clearly tell us that we need to shine our faith wherever we go, and in doing so, we will glorify God.

I want to describe two types of people. The first type is so heavily focused on their own life, desires and advancements that they act as though everyone around them are solely there to be at their beck and call. They have very little patience for anyone else and usually let them know about it, too. The second type of person is focused on what they can do for others. They have plenty of tolerance for others and they stay quiet instead of lashing out when things don't go right. I'm sure as I described these two types of people, names of each example popped in your head, hopefully more of the second type. We all have the freedom to choose which type of person we want to be. It's pretty easy to see which type of person honors God. You can't focus on yourself and others at the same time. Most likely, there are individuals all around us who could use some of Jesus. My prayer is that the Lord will show us how to shine His light on others. May we make it our goal today to make someone's life better by sharing the love of Christ with them. I'm thankful someone shared it with me.

Lord, please give us the eyes to see the opportunities to share You with others throughout our days. Amen.

65...TIZZY-FREE PLEASE

Good morning! Have you ever found yourself in a complete tizzy? You know, when you've pondered, contemplated, and looked at something from every angle possible, and mentally you've worn yourself plum out. Just to realize that not one thing is different than when this crazy roller coaster ride started... except now you are absolutely exhausted! Why, oh why, do we do this to ourselves??? If someone was to ask us if we were worried about something, we'd say, "No," and we'd say it with lots of conviction, too. I know this because I'm trying to find my way out of a tizzy now. In my situation, there are just so many things to consider, as I'm sure is true in your case also. But, I'm learning to recognize my tizzies quicker than I've done in the past.

What do we do when everything is crazy around us and we feel like we have to fix things, and fix them quickly? I'd like to put this next phrase on a canvas to be my reminder. "When in doubt, wait it out." Psalm 130:5 says, "I wait for the Lord, my soul does wait, and in His word do I hope." I know it's hard, but we need to hold steady until we see the path that God will open up and lay out for us before we make a move.

We waste so much energy on worrying ... or whatever we choose to call it. Instead, we need to listen to our internal GPS system and let the Lord's sweet voice guide us. So, the next time you realize you're about to get in a full blown tizzy, take time to get alone with the Lord. Confess that all your worrying goes against what God has taught us to do and then sit back and wait to see what God has in store because you know it's going to be good!

Heavenly Father, please help us skip the whole step of getting ourselves all worked up over issues out of our control. When we start to get in a tizzy, help us recognize what is going on and then please Holy Spirit, speak to us so we can put a stop to the craziness and just rest in You. Amen.

65

66...NO WORTHLESS THING

Good morning! Have you ever sat down at night and just wanted to watch a little TV but channel after channel offered you nothing but junk? And then you ask yourself why you are paying for all of those channels. I think that is one reason I like watching sports so much and why I'm loving watching the Olympics now because it gives me something decent to watch.

I thought about this when I was reading two verses in the Bible. Matthew 6:22 says, "The lamp of the body is the eye; if therefore your eye is clear, your whole body will be full of life." It's the whole garbage in, garbage out mentality. Whatever you set your eyes on are the things that you're going to be thinking about. So if you watch programs that would not be pleasing to God, those un-pleasing thoughts will rattle around in your head. Often, as those thoughts meander through your mind, the enemy is ever so happy to add to those thoughts and, before you know it, God is totally out of your thoughts and junk is totally filling your head!

So, are you up for a challenge??? As you go through your days, could you possibly focus on Psalm 101:3? "I will set no worthless thing before my eyes..." Instead of watching junk on TV, what if you grabbed a good book off the shelf to read? Better yet, what if you read THE "Good Book," the Bible?

We have to intentionally make the decision daily to not set our eyes upon anything unpleasing to the Lord. Whether it's a place we chose to go to, a movie we pick to see or a TV show, it's all about choice. My prayer for all of us is that we would honor our Lord and Savior by focusing on the things that would be pleasing to Him. Things that would help us and others grow in our spiritual walk.

Lord, help us to have the will power to not set anything worthless before our eyes as we want to honor You in all we do. Amen.

67...SWEET REMINDERS

Good morning! How has your week been? Sometimes, the happenings of our weeks just beat us down, don't they? When you're having one of those weeks, a little encouragement goes a long way. We just need to be reminded of who we are and to whom we belong.

My sister sent me a box of goodies this week. In the box was a precious book by Max Lucado titled, *God Thinks You're Wonderful!* Once again God's timing is perfect. He knew I needed some reminders of what I mean to Him. The book had cute reminders like if God had a wallet, my picture would be in it. If He had a refrigerator, my picture would be on it. Sweet little things to remind me of what I already know. God loves me ... always has, always will. But it was the reminder found in Isaiah 49:16 that will stick with me. "**Behold**, I have inscribed you on the palms of My hands…"

Do you remember when you were in school and you wanted to make sure that you remembered something, and you wrote it on the palm of your hand? That's kind of how I see this verse but with one huge difference. When we wrote notes on the palms of our hands, those reminders would only stay there until we washed our hands. But with God, our names are forever "inscribed" on the palm of His hands, never to be washed off.

"**Behold.**" As a son or daughter of the Lord Jesus Christ, this reminder of God loving us so much that our names are engraved on His hands should help us get through whatever life throws at us. So next time life tries to knock you down, remember that God thinks you're wonderful! With God on our side, we have all the love and encouragement that we'd ever need.

Jesus, thank You for the reminder that You love us enough to have our names as Believers inscribed on the palm of Your hand. Amen.

68...GOING FOR THE GOLD

Good morning! As I was watching the Olympics, the announcer made a comment that caused me to stop and think. These athletes work on their skills for four years. They spend countless hours perfecting each element needed to earn a place on the podium. They put their blood, sweat, and tears into training. They run their performance over and over in their head over those four years. They work so hard to get to the Olympics, and once there, when they take the ice, track, slope, etc., in a matter of minutes, their performance is over. All of that work for a once in four years chance to get a gold medal. Some of them rise to the challenge and earn that medal and others are so nervous that they can't give the performance they know is in them.

That reality made me stop and think about what we should be aspiring to do as a son or daughter of our Heavenly Father. Do we spend time preparing for what we have been called to do? Do we spend time in God's word to have scripture to back up our call? So, what is God calling us to do as Believers? Matthew 28:19 gives us the answer. "Go therefore and make disciples of all the nations, baptizing them in the name of the Father, and the Son and the Holy Spirit..."

This command isn't something we train to do once in every four years. God wants us to be ready to share the hope that we have in Jesus Christ on a daily basis, whenever the opportunity arises. We need to be prepared so our nerves don't stop us from sharing the faith that is within us. So, the question we need to answer is, "Are we prepared to share Jesus with those who have not secured their place on God's podium?" As Christians, we need to do whatever God calls us to do so we can help others walk on streets of gold in heaven for all eternity. So, here's to going for the gold!

Lord, help us be ready to share our faith in You with others whenever the opportunity presents itself. So thankful someone shared with me. Amen.

69...MOVING FORWARD

Good morning! The Bible study I'm currently doing is *No Other Gods* by Kelly Minter. In this Bible study she tells a story about a man that was interviewed on TV after Hurricane Katrina devastated New Orleans. She said that he was one of the few people that stayed even after the city had just been ravaged. His home had been flooded, there was no clean drinking water available, and there were dead bodies lying in the street. When the interviewer asked him why he remained, he said that he couldn't think of a better place they could take him than where he was.

This man couldn't say goodbye to his home because he couldn't envision that there was anything better for him out there. That story is so sad but as Christians we often do the same thing. We must always trust that God has something better for us than what we're trying to hang on to. Even if we can't imagine what could be better, by faith we need to believe that God knows what is best for us. Knowing that God knows best, why do we fight change in our life so much? I think it boils down to the fact that we find comfort in the familiar over the unknown.

So what familiarities are you trying to hold on to in your life? Is the Lord trying to change up your life through your job? Or maybe He is wanting to relocate you to a new home. Could it even be that He wants to bring a new relationship in your life? The unknown can be scary, but it doesn't have to be if you take the Lord with you. Psalm 23 is a beautiful song of trust. Verse 3 says, "He restores my soul; He guides me in the paths of righteousness for His name's sake." God only wants the best for us, so instead of fighting the unknown, my prayer for us is that we would truly trust God to lead us in the ways He knows are best. Here's to trusting the Lord and enjoying the path He takes us on.

Lord, please help us to see that we can't move forward if we aren't willing to let go of what we have. Give us the courage to say "yes" to what You have for us. Amen.

70...NOT OUR FIGHT

Good morning! One of the hardest lessons I've learned as I've grown in my faith in the Lord is talked about in Ephesians 6:12. "For our struggle is not against flesh and blood, but against the rulers, against the powers, against the world forces of this darkness, against the spiritual forces of wickedness in the heavenly places."

Life throws us all kinds of curve balls. When someone is intentionally trying to make our lives miserable our flesh wants to jump in there and fight it out. I don't know how many times in my life the Lord has tapped me on the shoulder and reminded me that this (whatever the problem was at that time) is not my battle. And most of the time I'd say "ok" and let Him fight for me. But there have been times that I've tried to convince God that I can fight this one myself, just because my flesh really wanted to take a swing at the curve ball. I don't know how God talks to you but with me He often just repeats what He's already said. In these cases, He just said again, "This is not your battle." Reluctantly, I'd say ok and turn it over to Him, but this act of obedience might now come immediately.

We look at the person causing all the grief as the problem, but they aren't the problem at all. As Believers, our enemies are the demonic hosts of Satan and they are always ready for mortal combat. And they might do a bang-up job trying to wreck our lives so that we'd be rendered useless for God but once we say ok to God and let Him fight our battles, the victory is always His!! So, the next time someone is causing you lots of pain and heartache, just remember that the sooner we turn the problem and the person causing it over to God, the sooner the battle waged against you will be won. And we know that God has a winning record - 100% of the time! Here's to being on the winning team!

Lord, thank You for fighting our battles. Amen.

71...BILLY GRAHAM

Good morning! Choices ... we all have to make thousands of them every day. I was thinking about the choices in life as I remembered the life of Billy Graham, who entered heaven yesterday. This quote from him sums up his life perfectly. "My one purpose in life is to help people find a personal relationship with God, which, I believe, comes through knowing Christ." He made the choice to spend his time seeking to bring Jesus to as many people as possible. Dr. Graham spent his life traveling the world sharing the Good News of Jesus Christ. One of the things I loved about him is that he never sugar-coated anything about Jesus. He preached the word of God and made no apologies for it. He told you like it was and that is something we all need to hear ... the truth. News stories estimate that Dr. Graham's 99 years on earth brought millions of people to the Lord. I'm sure his journey had struggles, just like ours, but he never forgot why God put him here on earth. He, like all of us, have a job to do and he did it well. I was thinking about the struggles he might have had as I read Galatians 6:9-10.

> Let us not lose heart in doing good, for in due time we will reap if we do not grow weary. So then, while we have opportunity, let us do good to all people, and especially to those who are of the household of the faith.

That verse reminded me of two things. First, as long as we are breathing, we have the opportunity to make choices to do good to others, and sharing Jesus is one of the ways to do good. And the second thing is that we are told to especially do good to other Believers. When the Lord calls us home, what will others say about the choices we made in our life? Did the choices we make have an eternal difference in the lives of others? Were others drawn to God because of the life we lived? For Dr. Graham, the answers to those questions would be a resounding, "Yes!" Without a doubt, I know God called Billy Graham one of His good and faithful servants and welcomed him home with open arms. My prayer for us is that we follow in his footsteps.

Lord, thank You for the life of Billy Graham. Amen.

72...I'LL PUSH YOU

Good morning! I just finished reading a book a friend of mine told me about called *I'll Push You*. It's an amazing story of two friends, Justin and Patrick, that make an intentional choice to live life out together. Leaving their wife and kids at home, these two friends embark on a 500-mile hike through the famous Camino de Santiago, a spiritual pilgrimage through the mountains of Spain. Oh yes, I almost forgot, Justin has a progressive neuromuscular disease that has left him unable to use his body, even his arms and legs. He needs help doing everything, including getting in and out of his wheelchair. It's an amazing book and one I would highly recommend, but only if you're willing to put pride aside and let God change you.

I now understand why my girlfriend suggested this book. In the twenty months that Alan has been in heaven, I have had to swallow my pride and let others help me take care of things that I couldn't do myself. In my areas of weakness, God has shown Himself strong. This story is such an amazing example of Galatians 6:2. "Bear one another's burdens, and thereby fulfill the law of Christ."

This story shows what happens when we intentionally make the needs of others more important than our own needs. That is exactly what Jesus tells us we are to do, and His life was the perfect example of that. The thing I need to remember is that when others help me, especially the help I didn't ask for, but God knew I needed, I need to graciously accept it and lay my pride aside. When I deny someone the opportunity to help me, I am denying them joy in life. I don't think that old adage, it's better to give than receive, is

right. I'm thinking both sides of the give/receive coin are important. Wow, you know a book is good when it causes you to think this much about it!

Lord, my pride often gets in the way of You meeting my needs. Help me lay it aside. Amen.

73...SING HIS PRAISES

Good morning! When I looked up the word stereotype on my phone, this is the definition I got. "A widely held but fixed and oversimplified image or idea of a particular type of person or thing." Stereotypes usually have a negative connotation associated with them. Things like the mental abilities of someone who has blonde hair, or unfortunately, how some see Christians as unhappy people, calling them hypocrites. You can't do anything about what color hair you were born with but there's a lot you can do about the negative imagines that are often associated with being a Christian.

Christians should be the happiest people walking on the face of this earth! We serve a God who created everything we find here on earth and as good as that is, He's also prepared a place for us in heaven for all eternity. God sent His only Son to earth to pay our sin debt so we could be free through Him. We have a hope that nonbelievers don't have. Although everyone has trials, as Believers we have a God to take refuge in. Psalm 5:11-12 says,

But let all who take refuge in You be glad, let them ever sing for joy; and may You shelter them, that those who love Your name may exalt in you. For it is You who blesses the righteous man, O Lord, You surround him with favor as with a shield.

We have the favor of Jesus. Just that fact alone should cause us to do cartwheels of joy (or at least a good hearty "woo-hoo" for all of us cartwheel-challenged individuals). Circumstances in life can be challenging and often overwhelming and dealing with those issues alone can drag us down and suck the joy right out of us. But God never intended for us to go it alone. He wants us to take refuge in Him and in spite of our circumstances to stay joyful. We can do this by keeping our eyes fixed on Jesus instead of our circumstances and singing praises to His name. Oh, and an occasional cartwheel will make God smile, too. So, here's to busting those stereotypes and spreading happiness!

Lord, help us to stay joyful regardless of our situation because having You on our side is all we need to sing Your praises. Amen.

74...GOD'S FRUIT

Good morning! Do you ever crack yourself up by looking back at your thought processes?? My mind can jump all over the place and then God brings those thoughts back and ties them up neatly with a bow, which then become my morning devotions. Today's devotion is no different.

I was recently talking with my mother and father in-law about bananas. I went to their house to drop something off just as my mother in-law was unloading groceries. As she was unpacking her bags, I noticed she only had two bananas. I said, "Wait, how did you only get two bananas in that bunch??" She said she always just breaks off how many she wants. I always buy the whole bunch and then try to figure out how to eat them before they get rotten, which is usually a problem. A person can only make so many loaves of banana nut bread.

Thinking about how to make fruit last got me thinking about the fruits we should have as Christians. You know, the ones listed in Galatians: love, joy, peace, patience, kindness, goodness, faithfulness, gentleness, and self-control. And then that reminded me of what Jesus said in John 15:16:

> *"You did not choose Me but I chose you, and appointed you that you would go and bear fruit, and that your fruit would remain, so that whatever you ask of the Father in My name He may give to you. This I command you, that you love one another."*

And the next thing that popped in my head was how to keep my fruit from going bad. God took all those thoughts bouncing around in my head and tied a nice, neat bow around them to give me the one thought to hold on to, and here it is. **You can't love if your fruit is rotten.** And there you have it. My thought process wrapped up in a morning text. As we go through our day, my prayer is that we will focus on God's fruit!

Lord, help our spiritual fruit grow...love, joy, peace, patience, kindness, goodness, faithfulness, gentleness, and self-control. Amen.

74

75...BEING ACCEPTED

Good morning! As I was reading two of my favorite verses in the Bible, Proverbs 3:5-6, I noticed something. When I turn to that chapter in Proverbs, I instinctively start with verse 5. But today, I started at the first verse and wondered why it took me so long to figure out that those verses that lead up to verse five and six are powerful, too.

Proverbs 3:1-4 says,

> *"My son, do not forget my teaching, but let your heart keep my commandments; for length of days and years of life and peace they will add to you. Do not let kindness and truth leave you; bind them around your neck, write them on the tablet of your heart. So you will find favor and good repute in the sight of God and man."*

Wow, now those are some amazing promises for us to hold on to! Who doesn't want to find favor with God and man? It's one of those basic needs in life we all long for...to find favor, or another way to say it is to be accepted.

These first four verses promise us that if we keep God's commandments in our hearts, the rewards are great ... length of days and years of life and peace they will add to us. And if we live a life where we show kindness to others and keep God's truth found in Scripture, we will find the favor not only of God but also man.

With all that being said, staying in God's word every day becomes even more important. Our Bibles should be our most prized possession on earth because through God's Word, we find out who He is and how He wants us to live out our lives. Here's to showing kindness to others as we keep the truth of the Lord in our hearts.

Lord, thank You for all the promises we find in Scripture. Help us understand the importance of staying in Your Word daily. Amen.

76...FEARING THE LORD

Good morning! As I read Psalm 34:8-10, I was reminded of a time I didn't understand what it meant to fear the Lord.

Oh taste and see that the Lord is good; how blessed is the man who takes refuge in Him! O fear the Lord, you His saints; for those who fear Him, there is no want. The young lions do lack and suffer hunger; but they who seek the Lord shall not be in want of any good thing.

Fearing the Lord doesn't mean that God is someone we need to run and hide from because we fear His wrath. Many think God is just waiting and watching for them to mess up and do something wrong so He can judge them, but nothing could be further from the truth. God loves us enough that He sent His only Son to earth to die for our sins. As Believers, because of the shed blood of Jesus Christ, when God looks at us, He sees us covered in clothes of righteousness.

Fearing the Lord means that as Believers, we should have a reverence for Him ... respecting Him by obeying His command-ments, submitting to His plan for our lives, and just being in awe of who He is and what He has done for us. Are we always going to get everything in our life right? Absolutely not, but as Believers we have no reason to be afraid of God when we fall short of the mark. God has promised us in Romans 8:38-39 that NOTHING can separate us from His love. He also told us in Hebrews 13:5 that He will NEVER leave us or forsake us. So, as we go about our day, mistakes and all, let's fear the Lord and bask in His awesomeness because He is worthy to be praised!

Heavenly Father, thank You for teaching us what it means to fear You. Thank You that Your Word reminds us that You will never leave us and that nothing can separate us from Your love. We praise You for who You are and what You have done for us. We praise You and give You our love. Amen.

77...FAITH LIKE GIDEON

Good morning! What do you do when life's challenges are just so overwhelming? The story of Gideon found in Judges Chapter 7, gives us the answer. In this story, God instructed Gideon to lessen the number of men who were there to fight to deliver Israel from the hand of Midian so they would not become boastful, thinking they won this victory by their own strength. Gideon started out with 32,000 men. God had him reduce his troops down to only 300 men. And then God used those few hundred men to defeat the camp of Midian, whose army was four times bigger than Gideon's.

The reason for that victory was that Gideon trusted God even though the numbers were not in his favor. That kind of trust in God doesn't happen overnight and it can't be obtained by just reading a book about faith. Gideon-style trust comes from life experiences. It's a process that takes place over time. Each time you trust God, your faith in Him increases. And God uses those difficulties in our lives to make us stronger in our faith. When the odds are against us, that's when the Lord shows His awesome power and delivers us from our challenges, in His perfect time and in His way.

Although God's ways sometimes don't make sense to us, we can have all the faith in the world in Him because of past times when He showed us His faithfulness in our circumstances. He delights in showing His strength in the midst of our weaknesses. In 2 Corinthians 12:9, Jesus says, "My grace is sufficient for you, for power is perfected in weakness." What overwhelming circumstances are you facing in your life? No matter what they are, in our weakness and inadequacies, we can be confident in the fact that God will show *His* faithfulness to those who trust Him. So, here's to having faith like Gideon and then watching God show Himself mightily in our situations.

Heavenly Father, thank You for the example of Gideon-style faith. Remind us that when we are weak, You are strong. Please show Yourself mightily in our lives. Amen.

78...HE'S ENOUGH

Good morning! I was recently talking with someone I dearly love and the question that came up was, "Is Jesus enough?" Is He enough to heal me? Is He enough to keep me safe in this crazy world we live in? Is He enough to mend my broken heart? Is He enough to help stretch my finances? Let me answer those questions by reminding us about a story found in Matthew 8:23-27. "When He got into the boat, His disciples followed Him. And behold, there arose a great storm on the sea, so that the boat was being covered with waves; but Jesus Himself was asleep. And they came to Him and woke Him saying, "Save us, Lord; we are perishing!" He said to them, "Why are you afraid, you men of little faith?" Then He got up and rebuked the winds and the sea and it became perfectly calm. The men were amazed, and said, "What kind of man is this, that even the winds and the sea obey Him?" Was Jesus enough then? What about when Jesus cast out the demons of two men in the country of the Gadarenes? (Matthew 8:28-34) Our how about when Jesus healed Peter's mother in-law? (Matthew 8:14-17) Or maybe when Jesus cleansed the leper? (Matthew 8:1-13) And those are just examples that are found in one chapter of the Bible.

Jesus must often shake His head at us. If we believe in the truth of John 3:16, "For God so loved the world, that He gave His only begotten Son, that whoever believes in Him shall not perish, but have eternal life," for our salvation, then why do we often have trouble believing Jesus is enough to handle our daily needs??? Jesus is enough for our earthly needs, like calming our stormy seas, as well as our eternal needs. We can trust Him for our small requests and for the requests that are bigger than we are. When we doubt Jesus' abilities, or when our faith isn't big enough to believe that

God can take care of our situation, we need to be like the father found in Mark 9:24, and declare, "I do believe; help my unbelief."

Lord, thank You that You are always, always enough! Amen.

79...GREENER ON THE OTHER SIDE

Good morning! We've all heard the phrase, "The grass is greener on the other side." I was thinking about this as I was watching my neighbor's cow twisting her neck and head to be able to eat the grass on the other side of the fence. In actuality, it's all the same grass, but in life the difference is our attitude about the grass.

What do we do then when we see the neighbor's grass as being better than ours? A quote from Angel Chernoff has a good answer. She says, "If the grass looks greener on the other side ... Stop staring. Stop comparing. Stop complaining. Start watering the grass you're standing on." I read that quote several times and my response each time was "Wow!"

What does God say about comparing our lives to others? Scripture after Scripture tells us that our lives are uniquely ours. When we compare our lives to others, we are wasting our time because God is taking us on a road that was paved just for us. Such comparisons lead to envying others, which is truly something God tells us not to do. The NIV version of Proverbs 14:30 explains why envying what others have is a bad idea. "A heart at peace gives life to the body, but envy rots the bones."

If you've ever been in a situation where it feels as though it is eating you alive, a.k.a. rotting your bones, then you'll understand what that verse means. Not one of us would willingly put ourselves in a situation that would be that detrimental to our lives. But Scripture tells us that when we are being envious of others, we are doing just that. So, my prayer is that we'd examine and rid our lives of envy and to always seek the Lord's peace in our lives, which gives life to the body.

Lord, help us focus on just our lives and not compare our lives with others. Help us focus on the path You've laid out specifically for me. Amen.

80...LONG-TERM RELATIONSHIP

Good morning! God has put in all of us the longing to be loved. And the older I get, the more I understand that it's not the length of a relationship that makes it so special but it's the openness of our lives and the lives of those we love that give us that deep rooted relationship. It's definitely quality over quantity.

There are people that I've known my entire life, but I don't really know them. I can't tell you what their favorite things are, the things that bring them joy, and for a lot of them, how they feel about the Lord. But I've been blessed with some new friendships lately and I know more about them and what makes them happy and how they feel about the Lord and it has all happened in a relatively short amount of time. Those are the relationships that will be lifelong. The good Lord has tied our hearts together. The same principles are true with our relationship with God. We can know about Him for our entire life, but if we don't allow our hearts to be connected to His, it'll be just like people that you've known your entire life but you have no real knowledge of anything more than the superficial things.

So how do you feel about long-term relationships? Jesus is reaching out to you to join Him in one. He will satisfy the greatest longing to be loved in your life. Psalm 107:9 says it this way. "And He has satisfied the thirsty soul, and the hungry soul He has filled with what is good." He has everything we long for. And He wants to give us this forever. If you don't have that long-term relationship going on with the Lord, you can start it today. Just invite Jesus into your heart by acknowledging you have a sin problem, knowing He is the only One that can take care of that issue. For the blood that He shed on Calvary will cover every sin; past, present, and future. God wants to be your everything from now throughout eternity. Praying today is the day you say "Yes" to the long-term relationship that Jesus offers.

Lord, thank You for the long-term relationship
You offer us! Amen.

81...LIVE LIKE YOU'RE LOVED

Good morning! As I was listening to the radio last night, lyrics to a song got me thinking. "Live like you're loved" were the words that got my attention. When others look at you, can they see that you are living like you're loved? We will get back to that question in a moment. I believe the best example of the word "love" can be found in John 3:16. "For God so loved the world, that He gave His only begotten Son, that whoever believes in Him shall not perish, but have eternal life." God is love and He loved us so much that He made a way for us to stand as righteous before Him through the shed blood of Jesus Christ.

Let's go back to my initial question. Knowing that God loved us enough to send His only Son so we could be set free and live like we're loved, what does that look like? 1 Peter 2:9 can help us with that answer. "But you are a chosen race, a royal priesthood, a holy nation, a people for God's own possession..." So as Believers, we are royalty. (Are you sitting up a bit straighter yet???) Should the insignificant things in life drag us down as though they are what defines us? Absolutely not! When is the last time you saw a news clip on TV where Queen Elizabeth was all slumped over with a doom and gloom expression on her face because somebody didn't like her or that something wasn't going perfect in her life? Those things don't change who she is or her position with the people of England. Using that example to give us a visual, let's apply that to our lives as children of God. We aren't defined by what others think of us, or by how smoothly our life is running, or by how much money we have in our checking account. We are defined by who God says we are. Romans 8:17 tells us that the Creator of all has made us joint heirs with Jesus Christ. That's how we are defined and that's how we should live! God loved us enough to send Jesus to die in our place so we could be set free by the bondage of sin. Being a child of God is what defines us, and living within that freedom given to us by the shed blood of Jesus Christ, is living like we're loved.

Lord, help us live a life like we are loved. Amen.

82...STRENGTHENING OUR CHAIN

Good morning! Every event in our lives becomes another link in the "chain of life" we all have. Some links are good and some, well, not so much, but they all link together and have helped us become the person we are today. With the good links, we rejoice. With the bad links, we can still rejoice as there are many lessons to be learned through trying times and through those lessons, our chain gets stronger. The same thing is true with our faith. Every time we see God at work, our faith is bolstered, and we learn to trust Him even more.

Philippians 4:4 tells us to "Rejoice in the Lord always; again I will say, rejoice!" It's easy to rejoice when the link we are dealing with is a good one but how do we rejoice when the link is a bad one? For me, I can encourage myself by looking back at all the times that the Lord has carried me through and thus, strengthened me. I can just focus on how God brought good out of a bad situation.

When we rejoice, we are being obedient to the Lord. We are not ignoring the difficulties we are enduring, but we are choosing to acknowledge that God is able to handle our situation. Even though our hearts may be heavy with grief or sadness because of what we are facing, when we rejoice, we are saying that we have confidence that the Lord has this issue in His very capable hands and we are willing to keep our focus on Him. When all we are thinking about is how awesome God is and remembering all He has done for us, it becomes much easier to rejoice, even if we don't see the good in our current link. So, here's to strengthening our chain of life by relying on and trusting in our Lord.

Lord, thank You that with each link, You are strengthening our chain and our faith in You. Help us to keep rejoicing regardless of our situation. Amen.

83...CRAZY ABOUT HIM

Good morning! Have you had a time in your life that you felt like things were just spinning out of control, where you just wanted to slam on the brakes, so you could take a deep breath? I'll come back to this question in a minute.

My brother and his wife are in town for a visit. When they pulled in my driveway, I opened the garage door to let them in. As soon as my dog saw who was here, he started running around in circles. Cope was running so fast through the garage that he slid and wiped out on the concrete. That only slowed him down for a second though. Once Cope regained his footing and caught his breath, he was off again. I think he ran more in those minutes than he had in days. My family sure knew he was glad to see them!

Now back to my original question. When you're trying to stay afloat and are trying to just breathe, do you run to God for help? Hopefully you do. You ask Him for relief from whatever is spinning out of control in your life. You tell Him you just want the craziness to stop. And God wants us to bring all our concerns to Him. 1 Peter 5:7 says it this way. "Cast all your anxiety on Him, because He cares for you."

I think we are all pretty good at taking our problems to the Lord, but when is the last time that you showed God you were excited to see Him, like Cope did when my family pulled up? I'm not suggesting that you run around in circles in your garage and yard, but I am suggesting we make time to just love on the Lord. He has and is continuously doing so much for us. He deserves our praise. So, the next time you ask the Lord to help you with the craziness in your life, make sure you take time to let Him know you are crazy about Him.

Lord, we are crazy in love with You. Thank You for all You constantly do for us. We are grateful for it all. Amen.

84...THINGS OF THE HEART

Good morning! We've all heard the phrase, "You can't take it with you." This is referring to the fact that we won't be taking any of our earthly possessions with us when we pass away. So why do we focus so much on gaining material things when they are just temporary?

Keeping a heavenly perspective can help us live a more peaceful life. You know in life, fairly or unfairly, lots of things can be taken from you, like your money, or possessions. But if you trust God, He will replace anything that was taken from you that He knows you need. After all, everything on earth belongs to God and He can move things around any way He sees fit. Philippians 4:19 says, "And my God will supply all your needs according to His riches in glory in Christ Jesus."

So again, it's not the "things" that matter in our lives. The only things on this earth that can't be taken from us are the things that reside in our heart. Our love for God the Father, God the Son, and God the Holy Spirit, are a few of those things. Other things that reside in our heart are the love we have for one another and the memories we've collected over the years.

Hopefully, we also carry forgiveness in our hearts. Sometimes this is hard to do, especially when it's crystal clear that you were wronged or taken advantage of. The Lord will deal with those things. Our job is to forgive and move on. Trust me, I know this is much harder to do than say. It's a choice we have to make though. Because the Lord has forgiven us, we have to forgive, too. So, since we can only take things of the heart with us to Heaven,

 my prayer for us is that our primary focus in life will be of heavenly things and that we will not concern ourselves with the rest.

Lord, please help us learn to focus on only things of the heart and let the rest of the stuff go. Amen.

85...FINISHING WELL

Good morning! In so many things in life, it's not how you begin something that is important, it's how you end it. As I was watching tennis, I thought about the verse in Hebrews 12:1. "And let us run with endurance the race that is set before us..." In the tennis match that I was watching, one of the players started out strong but as the third and final set started, that player pretty much just gave up on the match. There are no prizes for a great start. Only a great finish will allow you to reap the benefits. Again, it wasn't how he started that will be remembered from that match, it's how he finished the match by just giving up.

The same is true in our Christian walk. Life is short and we should want to live it well. We only have one shot at this life, and since there are no do-overs, we have to live an intentional life for Christ. As I was thinking about this, Billy Graham came to mind. Despite the fact that his body was failing him, he still finished well. He served the Lord, and served Him well, for over 70 years. He was 94 years old when he published one of his last books in 2013, *The Reason for My Hope*. His life reminds me that regardless of our age or our health, there is always something we can do to serve the Lord. Dr. Graham could have retired in his later years and said that he had done his part and only focused on himself. But instead, He continued to run the race that God set before him, and because of that, many, many lives were changed and now he is reaping the eternal rewards for finishing well.

So how are you doing in the race that God has set before you? Are you on track to finish well or have you given up? There will always be speed bumps along the way. Even though they might slow us down, they don't have to end our race. With God's help, we can stay the course and finish well and that's my prayer for all of us.

Lord, help us to finish the race You have set out before us. Amen.

86...UNCONDITIONAL LOVE

Good morning! Does your pet show you more unconditional love than others in your life??? Hmmm ... Do you show others more unconditional love than your pet does??? Do you ever feel left out when you thought for sure you'd be included??? We all want to be included and loved unconditionally but that doesn't always happen.

So, then what do we do when others step on our toes? The first thing we need to do is forgive them for causing us pain. And although that is sometimes a really hard thing to do, we still need to do it. Secondly, we need to ask the Lord what He wants us to learn through this hurt. And finally, we need to look at things with a new perspective.

Psalm 63:3-5 says,

> *"Because Your lovingkindness is better than life, my lips will praise You. So I will bless You as long as I live; I will lift up my hands in Your name. My soul is satisfied as with marrow and fatness, and my mouth offers praises with joyful lips."*

We can't be praising God at the same time we are focusing on the pain that someone is causing us. *JOY*ful lips are those that put *J*esus first, *O*thers second and *Y*ourself last.

It's true that others might not always consider us, our wishes, or our feelings above their own, but that isn't how it should be. We need to put others ahead of ourselves. By putting Jesus and others before our own needs, our attitude and perspective will line up with the Lord's and that is absolutely the best place to be.

So, the next time someone causes you pain, step away from the situation long enough that you and the Lord can work through it. Then when you are with that person the next time, you'll be able to show them the same love God shows you ... unconditional love.

Lord, help us show others the same unconditional love that You show us. Help us to not focus on any wrong that has been done to us and focus on loving like You do. Amen.

87...SPRING FORTH

Good morning! I woke up this morning to the sounds of birds singing outside. The calendar tells us that today is the first day of spring. For many, this is a day that they've been looking forward to for some time now. The bitter cold, winter days are over and the freshness of spring is in the air. I've been watching the birds on my bird feeders show signs of spring, too. The yellow finches that were so pale throughout the winter are now turning a more vibrant yellow. The jonquils are blooming, and green is popping up everywhere. It's refreshing to see more new life spring forth every day.

As I enjoy the beautiful nature outside that God has provided, I began looking at the new birth that God is bringing forward inside of me. I have recently gone through a season in my life where it was often hard to see God's beauty in everything. But as He is bringing me out of that season, I feel new life within me. A couple of Bible verses that really spoke to me over this period of time was Lamentations 3:22-23. "The Lord's lovingkindness indeed never cease, for His compassions never fail. They are new every morning; great is Your faithfulness."

We serve such a compassionate God. No matter what season of life you are currently in, with God, each day can be like the first day of spring. We can feel a refreshing in our soul as each new day begins. We can get rid of the mistakes of yesterday, as they don't have to be repeated. Each new day with the Lord brings with it new hope. So, as we go through this day, my prayer for us is that we watch to see what new life God wants to spring forth in our souls.

Heavenly Father, You are such a caring and compassionate God. You give us a new start each day where we can leave the undesirable things of yesterday in the past and move forward. Thank You for the new hope You give us daily. Amen.

88...BOUNDARIES

Good morning! In 2 Peter 1:5-7 we are given some guidelines to help us to grow in Christian virtue.

Now for this very reason also, applying all diligence, in your faith supply moral excellence, and in your moral excellence, knowledge, and in your knowledge, self-control, and in your self-control, perseverance, and in your perseverance, godliness, and in your godliness, brotherly kindness, and in your brotherly kindness, love.

And in verse 11, Peter writes that if we practice these things in life, we will never stumble.

Of that list, self-control is the area I'm currently working on. Self-control takes work. We must make a choice about whatever we are dealing with. Self-control is not isolated to just things that we would all deem bad. Self-control still needs to be used on those things that are good. For example, we all need food to survive but without self-control we can indulge in too much food or the wrong kinds of food for us. That's my challenge these days. I'm trying to stay within my dietary guidelines. Some days I do a great job with this, other days, not so much.

If I'd just remember that God has given me everything I need to live life within necessary boundaries, I'd understand that making the choice to exercise self-control is something I can do each and every time I'm tempted to cross the boundary lines. Are you struggling with any self-control issues? If so, just remember that God can help you overcome those struggles. Like with everything else, with the Lord's help, we can win the self-control battle, day by day, one step at a time. And for that, I'm very thankful!

Lord, thank You for giving us boundaries in life. They help us stay within what is best for us. And thank You for Your help in our struggles with self-control. With Your assistance, we can win that battle. Amen.

89...BELONGING TO HIM

Good morning! Have you ever just sat down and opened your Bible and the words practically jump off the page at you? That's what happened with me yesterday. I opened to Psalm 103. I'm sure I've read these verses many times, but yesterday it seemed like I was reading those verses for the first time. Psalm 103:1-5 says,

> *Bless the Lord, O my soul, and all that is within me, bless His holy name. Bless the Lord, O my soul, and forget none of His benefits; who pardons all your iniquities, who heals all your diseases; who redeems your life from the pit, who crowns you with lovingkindness and compassion; who satisfies your years with good things, so that your youth is renewed like the eagle.*

It was the last part of verse two that jumped off the page for me..."and forget none of His benefits." I'm not sure we could ever list all the benefits of belonging to God because there are so many. When we become a child of God, we enter into His family. When we become God's child upon accepting the gift of salvation through Jesus Christ, all the benefits of being the Lord's are ours. He forgives all our sins...past, present, and future. He takes our broken lives and turns them into something special, as only He can do. It's mind boggling to try to think through all the benefits of belonging to Him. There is no other relationship like the one we have with our Heavenly Father in all the universe. He loves us unconditionally. We attempt to love others unconditionally, but we fall short of that all the time. With God, that is a constant that we can always count on if we belong to Him. There's no better time to reflect on all the benefits that come with belonging to the Lord. Being a child of God gives us so much to be thankful for and that is the Good News worth sharing.

Heavenly Father, the benefits of being Your child are too numerous to count. You have given us all these things and we don't deserve one of them. You truly love us unconditionally and for that we are so grateful. Amen.

90...TABLE TIME

Good morning! I can't get my pastor's message from Sunday out of my mind, which is actually a good thing. He spoke on Psalm 23:5. In that verse, we are told that God has prepared a banquet at His table just for each of us who are Believers. "You prepare a table before me in the presence of my enemies." My pastor's words created a beautiful visual of God and me (or you) just sitting down for a meal and sharing life. It's a picture I want to carry with me always.

God wants to dine with us. He's asking us to sit down and share our hearts with Him. He's encouraging us to spend some quality one-on-one time. It's mind-boggling when you think about it. The Creator of Heaven and Earth wants to spend time just talking with us. What would your dinner conversation be like with the Lord? Would you talk about all the blessings He's given you? Would you share your hurts, as well as your dreams? Would you ask for His guidance in the circumstances of your life? The great news is that we can dine daily with the Lord through His Word and by setting aside some "table time" each day with Him. As we read Scripture, the Lord will make His words come alive for us. It's a gift that keeps on giving. We just need to receive it daily.

My pastor had a one-liner that I'm going to use to remind myself that my first conversation of my day needs to be with the Lord. He said, "I want to get to the Word before the world gets to me." That is so true! Our enemies try to mess with us on a regular basis, so if we want to defeat them, with God's help, we need to daily feast on God's word. If we can have a table conversation with the Lord to begin our day, the doors that our enemies try to enter through, to cause havoc in our day, will be closed because their darkness can't survive in God's Light. So, here's to pulling up a chair and spending some time dining with God.

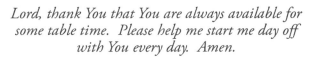

Lord, thank You that You are always available for some table time. Please help me start me day off with You every day. Amen.

91...BLESS THE REST

Good morning! The "unexpected" can sometime derail us but other times, it's a nice surprise. Take yesterday for example. March 20 was the first day of spring but mid- morning, about 30 minutes before it officially became spring, it started snowing. I had to just laugh. When stuff happens like that, I call them God winks. It's as though He is just reminding us Who is in control. It's Him, not the calendar. And the same is true in our lives. God is in control even though we often think that the control is in our hands.

There are so many verses in the Bible that discuss God being in charge. One of my favorites is Romans 8:28. "And we know that God causes all things to work together for good to those who love God, to those who are called according to His purpose." When we are in the middle of a difficult situation, we often forget to just take a deep breath and remind ourselves that God has this. We don't have to concern ourselves with taking the lead. Instead, we need to be a better follower.

During the winter Olympics, I remember an interview of a lady who participated in the half-pipe. She had a very challenging run with difficult weather conditions and the interviewer asked her how she kept her cool during her run. She said, "I don't always do this, but I did it today. I've learned to do all I can and then bless the rest." Those were some wise words she spoke. God expects us to do what we can do and leave the rest to Him. We can have total confidence that the Lord keeps His promises ... ALL of them. With that blessed assurance, we can get through even the most challenging times. So, the next time that you feel yourself getting worked up over a situation, take the time to step back and take a deep breath. Then be wise like the Olympian.
Do what you can and bless the rest.

Lord, thank You that You have our lives under control. Please help us to do what we can and leave the rest up to You. Amen.

92...HAVE IT HIS WAY

Good morning! I spent a really fun afternoon with my family this past Sunday. My great niece, who just turned two, was here. As part of her birthday gift, I gave her a bubble wand. My brother took her out on the deck to use it. My brother held his hand over hers and was showing her how you pull the wand out of the bottle of bubbles and then wave the wand back and forth to make all kinds of bubbles. It was cute but not how my sweet little great niece wanted to do it. After a few times my brother's way, she stepped away from him and did it her way. She pulled the wand out of the bottle and blew on it to create her bubbles. True, she didn't create as many bubbles but she was satisfied with her technique.

As I watched the video again that I took of them on the deck, it dawned on me that no one had to show that precious little thing how to do it her own way. She just pulled away and did it. I started humming the old Burger King jingle... "hold the pickle, hold the lettuce, special orders don't upset us ... have it your way..." (You can thank me later for putting that tune in your head today!)

Seriously though, don't we do the same thing in our Christian walk? We often ignore God's sovereignty because we think our way is better. Over time, and as we mature in our faith, we have a better understanding of the peace that comes with living under God's sovereign control. God's word tells us in Ephesians 4:6 that there is "one God and Father of all who is over all and through all and in all." God has total control and authority over every single thing in the universe, and the universe itself. With that being the case, wouldn't it make sense to yield our lives to the One that is sovereign over all? It's the best way to live a peaceful life. So, here's to letting God have it His way.

Lord, we are all too often wanting to have things in life our own way. Please help us see that You always have the best way and help us yield to Your control. Amen.

93...I CAN ONLY IMAGINE

Good morning! As we are quickly approaching Good Friday, I've been reflecting on the reason it was even needed. Sometimes I think we don't fully understand the costs of our sins. Maybe it's because we've never seen blood shed to atone for them. We're living in New Testament times, so we don't have to sacrifice animals like they did in the Old Testament and we weren't there when Jesus died for our sins. Even though we weren't physically there at Calvary, our sins were. Ephesians 1:7 says, "In Him we have redemption through His blood, the forgiveness of our trespasses, according to the riches of His grace." Jesus gave His life to bring complete forgiveness of our sins. He paid a price He didn't owe, and we owed a price because of our sins that we could not pay. I'm thankful for this gift that is given to us as Believers as I know it's something that I could never earn or deserve. I recently saw the movie "I Can Only Imagine." In the lyrics of the Mercy Me song with the same title, it poses the question of what we will do when we finally see Jesus face-to-face.

Surrounded by You glory, what will my heart feel
Will I dance for you Jesus, or in awe of You be still?
Will I stand in your presence, or to my knees will I fall?
Will I sing hallelujah, will I be able to speak at all?
I can only imagine ...

I've been thinking about what I would do when I see my Lord in person. I know I'd want to hug Him and thank Him for the gift of redemption, but what words could be adequate to express my gratitude? What I can do is try to live my life here in a way to honor Him. And when I sin, to ask for forgiveness. A forgiveness that was paid for by a sacrifice that's hard to fathom. What a love He has for us. I can only imagine...

Lord, thank You doesn't seem enough, but it's all I
have. Amen.

94...GOD'S GIFT OF PEACE

Good morning! Have you ever had a time in your life that was just so emotionally and/or physically draining and all you wanted was some peace? I'm pretty sure it is safe to say that we've all been there at one point or another. That much needed peace we are seeking during those times is a gift from God. I think we see by Jesus' own example that peace is something He wants for all of us, and not just during the trying times in life, but every day. In John 20:19 we find Jesus' words to His disciples after His resurrection and when He appeared to them for the first time. "So when it was evening on that day, the first day of the week, and when the doors were shut where the disciples were, for fear of the Jews, Jesus came and stood in their midst and said to them, 'Peace be with you.'" Of all the things Jesus could have said to His disciples, He went to the heart of what they needed … peace.

The older I get in my faith, the more I find myself praying simpler but more powerful prayers. At church this week, I was talking to a girlfriend of mine that has a lot on her plate right now. Both of her parents have been having significant health issues. They've been in and out of the hospital and even had to spend some time recouping at a nursing home. I told her that I would continue to pray for all of them. As I got alone with the Lord to pray for her family, I remembered what Jesus said to His disciples to give them what they needed to calm their anxieties. They needed the same thing my girlfriend needs … God's gift of peace.

As I pray for others, many times I ask the Lord to cover them with His peace. I just like that visual of the Lord wrapping them up in His peace blanket. I can envision their stress, fears, anxiety, pain and sorrow just melt away once His blanket is on them. It's a feeling of relief like nothing else can provide.

Lord, help us as we lift others up to You to
remember to pray to the heart of what they need
… Your peace. Amen.

95...TICKET TO PARADISE

Good morning! I am often blown away by technology. Last night was a good example of that. My sister and her husband were flying from California back to their home in Texas. I sent her a text that I thought she'd receive once she landed in Texas, but she responded to my text within a minute of me sending it ... from the plane! The ticket she bought allowed her to be connected to Wi-Fi. Now that's the kind of ticket I want to buy when I fly! Her ticket made me think about the ticket my pastor preached about yesterday ... the ticket to heaven.

My pastor talked about some of the things we'd experience in heaven. He described the beauty we'd see there. Things like walking on streets of gold and entering through gates made of pearls. He talked about the holy atmosphere we'd live in there. I can't even imagine what it will be like living in a place where there could be no sin ... none! And then of course, there's all the people who will be in Heaven. We'd once again be able to see loved ones that have entered Heaven before us. And how cool will it be to see and talk to those people we read about in the Bible? But nothing could top being able to be in the presence of the Lord once we're there. The more my pastor talked, the more I thanked God for giving me the blessed assurance of knowing that I already have my ticket to Heaven. It didn't cost me anything, but cost Jesus everything.

Jesus tells us in John 14:6 that He is "the way, and the truth, and the life." He continues by saying that, "no one comes to the Father, but through Me." So, if the only way to Heaven is through Jesus, and if Jesus is offering you a free ticket to go there, why wouldn't you accept it? As my pastor asked yesterday, what part of Heaven wouldn't you want to experience? It's definitely a question we all need to answer for ourselves. Praying you say yes to Jesus and secure your ticket to Paradise!

Jesus, thank You for paying for my ticket to heaven. Amen.

96...BUMP IN THE ROAD

Good morning! Yesterday was my first day going back to cardio rehab at the hospital. I'll be going three days a week for several months in hopes to help my heart get stronger. As I was doing the necessary paperwork, I was asked a bunch of questions about how I felt about things in life and how important certain things are to me in my life. As I was honestly answering the questions the best way I knew how, I was reminded of what I can't do and what I don't have. Within a few minutes of that reflection, I felt a wave of sadness come over me. It kind of froze me in my seat. You ever experience something like that? Anyway, I didn't stay that way long because I cracked myself up when I thought that if I stayed in that sadness, I'd have to change my answer about not being depressed... lol After they had me hooked up to the monitors, they had me walk six minutes around the track. As I walked, a question came to my mind. "Am I enough?" It took me a lap or two to realize that question came from God and not something random in my head. My silent response was, "Yes Lord, You are enough."

As I continued my walking, I tried to come up with as many reasons as possible to defend my answer of God being enough, reasons backed up by Scripture. I was surprised at how easily the Scriptures came to mind. The first verse that came to my mind was Philippians 4:19. "And my God will supply all your needs according to His riches in glory in Christ Jesus." It's impossible to have a need that God can't meet because the entire world and everything in it is at God's beck and call. Ok, that dealt with the physical and material things in life but what verse deals with how I feel on the inside? Then He reminded me of 2 Corinthians 4:17. "For momentary, light affliction is producing for us an eternal weight of glory far beyond all comprehension..." I'm thankful for being reminded that Scripture is there to help us or someone we love to get through a bump in the road.

Lord, thank You that Your words help us navigate this life. No matter how long our bumps in the road are, You are always enough. Amen.

97...REMOVE THE CLUTTER

Good morning! How many closets and storage areas do you have in your home? I am in the process of simplifying my "stuff." If I haven't used it in a year or more, good chance I'm not going to use it in the future. So, I am taking things that others could use to organizations that can pass the items on to someone in need. And if it isn't useful ... well, tomorrow is trash day.

I want to be a good steward of what God has entrusted to me. I'm not just talking about the material things in life. I'm referring to the things of the heart. When is the last time you decluttered your heart? You know, getting rid of those things that keep you from being all that God wants you to be. Fear, unforgiveness, anger, jealousy, disappointment, and resentment are all things that can clutter our hearts. This is by no means an inclusive list but it's enough to make the point. The reason it's bad to leave those things in our heart is that we are taking room away from what God wants to put in our hearts instead. Deuteronomy 6:5 tells us that we should "... love the Lord your God with all your heart and with all your soul and with all your might." We can't fulfill this command if we don't remove the clutter that's hanging out in our hearts.

How then do we remove what doesn't belong there? The only way I know how is by allowing the Holy Spirit to help you. We have to be willing to change. With a willing heart the Holy Spirit can take your fear and anger and replace it with God's peace. Unforgiveness will be taken away, leaving you with a forgiving heart. Jealousy, disappointment and resentment can be tossed out and replaced with a spirit of contentment. And the list could go on and on. So, here's to getting rid of the clutter and opening up our hearts.

Holy Spirit, please help us get rid of the stuff in our hearts that just clutter it up. With Your help, we can make room for the good stuff. Amen.

98...HIS EYES ON US

Good morning! Alan has been walking the streets of gold for twenty-two months today. Some days, I think of him off and on, and other days I can't think of much else. There's no rhyme or reason for why some days are like that. It's just what happens. I know I'm not alone in this because so many people dearly miss that man. Plain and simple, to know Alan was to love him. I was thinking about all the lives he touched in the years he was here with us. Alan is just going to be one of those unforgettable souls.

I started thinking about Alan this morning as I read 2 Chronicles 16:9. "For the eyes of the Lord move to and fro throughout the earth that He may strongly support those whose heart is completely His." Alan was one of those people that the Lord would have found as He looked to and fro.

There are two things I love about that verse. The first thing is that the Lord is looking for those that love Him. That means He always has eyes on us. To know that the Creator of all, the King of Kings and the Lord of Lords is looking upon me is about the most comforting thought I could have. I know I could be in no better hands.

The second thing that I love is that the verse tells us why God is looking for those whose hearts are His. "...that He may strongly support those whose heart is completely His." We all need others to support us as we go through life but what we can do for each other is limited. Those limitations go out the window where God is concerned. He wants to "strongly" support us and because He has no limitations, there isn't a better supporter out there. So, the next time you are looking for some support to get you through the tough times, look no farther than Almighty God because He offers us support like no one else can.

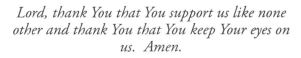

Lord, thank You that You support us like none other and thank You that You keep Your eyes on us. Amen.

99...MY SHELTER FOR LIFE'S STORMS

Good morning! We had a round of storms come through my area earlier this week. I typically enjoy thunderstorms, as long as there isn't any chance of a tornado. Well this week, I didn't enjoy the storms because, you guessed it, there were tornadoes. Thankfully none of them touched down here. I spent about thirty minutes in my storm cellar during the worst of the storm. I could really hear the hail and wind while I was in there, so I stayed until all I heard was rain. When I felt like it was safe to come out, I checked things around my place to see if there was any damage and I was very thankful not to see anything out of place.

As I sat in my storm cellar and waited out the storm, I did my best not to be anxious about having a need to be in the storm cellar, but I could feel it building inside of me. I was reminding the Lord that He spoke to storms and calmed them, and He also has calmed the storms in our lives. I told Him I'd really appreciate Him doing those things again. And thankfully, the storm let up about that time and I was able to go back inside. Since the storm had knocked out my satellite TV, I picked up the book I had been reading and opened the book to where my bookmark was and had quite a laugh. The page I was about to read had a point that the author, Max Lucado, wanted to drive home in a large, bold font. It said, "Anxiety is not a sin; it is an emotion. (So, don't be anxious about feeling anxious.)" How many times do we get stressed about being stressed? It's crazy, but we do it, or least I do from time to time. Instead of anxiety and stress, the Lord wants us to rely on Him and rest in His ability to handle the situation. I was reminded of Joshua 1:9. "Have I not commanded you? Be strong and courageous! Do not tremble or be dismayed, for the Lord your God is with you wherever you go." All I could say was "Yes, Lord," since I guess that the "wherever you go" means in storm cellars, too. Since I was reminded that God is my storm shelter, here's to doing it better with the next storm.

Lord, thank You for giving me all I need to
weather the storms in life. Amen.

100...HE KNOWS IT ALL

Good morning! As I was reading in Psalms this morning, I was comforted by the truth that the Lord knows everything about me. And since He is in total control, I'm in the best of hands. Psalm 139:1-5 says,

O Lord, You have searched me and know me. You know when I sit down and when I rise up; You understand my thought from afar. You scrutinize my path and my lying down, and are intimately acquainted with all my ways. Even before there is a word on my tongue, behold, O Lord, You know it all. You have enclosed me behind and before, and laid Your hand upon me.

There have been different times in my life, as I'm sure have been in yours, where I've struggled with life's circumstances. These times usually happened after major changes in my life, like the death of a loved one. During those times, I've often been at a loss of what I needed to do next in my life. But the good news is that the Lord knew every thought and concern that I'd have about the situation even before I was able to pose my first question to Him.

As I reflected on the verses that said, "You have enclosed me behind and before, and laid Your hand upon me," I started thinking about how God is tangibly doing that. For this current season I'm in, He has put people in my life that are able to give me Godly wisdom and direction, and as a result, things that once seemed overwhelming, now seem doable. And since the Lord has enclosed me behind and ahead, I know He will continue to move me down the path that He has cleared before me. So this morning, I can sit and take a deep breath with confidence because the God that knows everything about me, already knows what this day will bring. He knows how I will act and react to everything that happens in the course of my day. And knowing the Lord's hand is upon me, I know it'll be a beautiful day.

Lord, thank You for guiding me down the path You've laid out for me. Amen.

100

101...OUR CONSTANT HELPER

Good morning! Do you wear glasses? If so, aren't they there for a purpose? I'll get back to that in a minute. This morning I got up and with one eye open, one eye closed, I walked into my bathroom. Not fully wake yet, I grabbed my toothbrush, and a white tube which I thought was my toothpaste. I keep my toothbrush and my toothpaste in the same container as I keep the other things that I use in the morning to get ready for the day. Just so happens that the facial foam that I use to wash my face is also in a white tube, about the same size as my toothpaste. Needless to say, I now know that I need to go into the bathroom with both of my eyes open and my glasses on. I'm just sayin'! That eye-opening incident got me thinking about what else God gives us to use that we don't use correctly. For all of us that wear glasses, He has blessed us with better vision as a result of using them correctly, but it's up to us to decide to accept that help to have better vision by actually wearing them!

What does God give us in our Christian walk that we don't always use the way He intended? You know, things like the Bible, which is God's handbook for our lives. In order for us to get the desired results, we have to pick it up and read it. He also gives us other brothers and sisters in Christ who can offer Godly wisdom. But in order to receive that wisdom we have to be willing to open up and let them into our lives. Not the surface things of our lives, but the things of the heart. Knowing what we'd need, God intended us to use the gift I think we use the least … the Holy Spirit. Jesus tells us in John 16:7 that "It is to your advantage that I go away; for if I do not go away, the Helper will not come to you; but if I go, I will send Him to you. And He, when He comes, will convict the world concerning sin and righteousness and judgment…" We have been given the Holy Spirit as our constant Helper. He is always available, but how often do we turn to Him to receive the help we so desperately need? If you're like me, not nearly enough.

Holy Spirit, thank You for being our constant Helper. Forgive us for not coming to You more often when we need help. Amen.

101

102...PEACE IN GOD

Good morning! The Lord has been bringing me to verses about peace a lot lately. He knows I need to be reminded of the peace I can have in Him. And then in the Bible study I'm doing, the author talked about the difference between having peace "with" God and having peace "in" God. I've really never spent time thinking about the difference ... until now. We must have peace **with** God before we can have peace **in** God. Romans 5:1 tells us how we can have peace with God. "Therefore, having been justified by faith, we have peace with God through our Lord Jesus Christ ..." So peace with God comes when we've received Jesus as our Lord and Savior. Until we accept that gift of salvation, we are at odds with God because of our sin condition. Having peace with God is a one-time decision. After you've been covered by the blood of Jesus, that forgiveness will last for all eternity.

But having peace **in** God is a choice we have to make daily. It's a choice of the heart. We all know how crazy our lives can become. And if we try to do it alone, those pieces of craziness start stacking up on top of each other and they will eventually weigh us down. That's not how God wants us to live. He wants us to trust Him and let Him carry the load. I've learned that He has mighty big shoulders! Having peace **with** and **in** God has many benefits, but I really like the two found in John 14:27. "Peace I leave with you; My peace I give to you; not as the world gives do I give to you. Do not let your heart be troubled, nor let it be fearful." When we have both peace **with** God and peace **in** God, He says our hearts do not need to be troubled and we don't have to be afraid. I don't know about you but when things start spinning uncontrollably in my life or when fear tries to stop me in my tracks, those are my cues to get alone with the Lord and pass my load off to Him. Because of the peace God offers us, we can have a heart that is not troubled by the craziness in life and we can live a life that is not run by fear, and that is what I call a truly peaceful life!

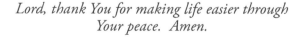

Lord, thank You for making life easier through
Your peace. Amen.

103...NO BETTER DAY THAN TODAY

Good morning! Life is so short. I'm reminded of that every time someone I love and care about passes away. One of our dear neighbors growing up died yesterday. He and his wife watched out for my brothers and sisters and I, especially after my mom died. They were the sweetest couple. I'm thankful he was given so many years of life here on this earth, 93 years to be exact, and that I know he is now with the Lord. Thinking about how short our life here is, I was reminded of James 4:14. "Yet you do not know what your life will be like tomorrow. You are just vapor that appears for a little while and then vanishes away." With that being the case, is there anything you have been putting off until a later date? Maybe there's a decision that needs to be made, or forgiveness you need to extend. Or maybe it's just making time to go visit an old friend. Whatever the case may be, today might just be the perfect day to take care of it.

Sometimes I don't think we understand the importance of getting the most out of our days and we operate on the "someday" model. You know, when we say, "Oh, I'll get around to it ... someday." There are some things that if we never got around to doing, it wouldn't be life altering. But there is a decision that if we never got around to making would impact our life forever, both here on earth and our life after we die. Since we are here for just a little while, like a vapor, we can't put the important things off to a "someday" down the road. If you haven't made the decision to accept Jesus as your Lord and Savior yet, I'd like to encourage you to not put it off another day. We are not guaranteed tomorrow but what we are guaranteed is that if we die before we made that most important decision, we will spend eternity separated from the Lord. So, let me ask you a question. If your road on earth ended today, would your family and friends be comforted knowing they'd see you again in heaven? Or would they say that you meant to get around to making your plans for eternity but time ran out?

Lord, for those that haven't made that decision, may today be the day they choose Jesus. Amen.

104...TRASH DAY

Good morning! Today is trash day for me. Where I live, everyone is responsible for getting their own trash service. Most neighbors have a large trash can from their trash provider that they roll down their driveway to the street once a week. My service just wants the trash to be put in trash bags and then they'll pick up the bags placed just outside my garage door. That's about as easy as it gets. Regardless of how it gets hauled off, there is action required on our part to get this chore taken care of.

Does spending time with God ever feel like a chore to be checked off your to-do list? Spending time alone with God takes action on our part. We must intentionally set aside time without distractions to learn and listen to what He wants to teach us. Preparing for this quiet time is a lot like taking out the trash. We have to remove the clutter going on in our head but forcing our minds to be still, takes practice. Jesus showed us how He did that in Mark 1:35. "In the early morning, while it was still dark, Jesus got up, left the house, and went away to a secluded place, and was praying there." We can't have that one-on-one time with God if we're trying to multitask ... watching the morning news, answering texts or emails we received the night before, checking Facebook, etc. Too often we want that time to come easy for us without any or much effort on our part. Like me just having to set my trash bag outside my garage door. It's as if we are telling God that He has just a couple of minutes during commercials to tell us anything He wants us to know that day. And when that commercial is over, we're up and getting another cup of coffee and going on with our morning routine feeling good that we were able to check off on our list that we spent time with God. And then we wonder why God doesn't speak to us. Have you ever just forgotten to take out the trash? That stench reminds me of what it's like when we don't set time aside for God. Our lives get cluttered with trash and that keeps us from growing in our relationship with Him. If it was important enough for Jesus to set aside time to be alone with the Father, then we need to follow His example.

Lord, help us to make our quiet time with You a
priority. Amen.

105...HE'S OVERCOME THE WORLD

Good morning! As much as we don't like it, we are going to have trials and tribulations in this world. The Lord didn't sugar-coat this when He talked about it in Scripture. In John 16:33, Jesus said, "These things I have spoken to you, so that in Me you may have peace. In the world you have tribulation, but take courage; I have overcome the world."

If you're like me, we too often put our focus on the trials and tribulation part of this verse. Maybe we do this because we are so familiar with the difficulties life can bring. But I want to get better at placing my focus on the two gold nuggets in this verse. The Lord loved us enough to put it out there in black and white. He said that we would 100%, absolutely, positively have difficulties in this life. And He told us that to give us a heads up on what was coming so we wouldn't be caught off guard when it happens.

No matter what kinds of trials you're facing, the Lord also told us we can have peace in Him because HE HAS OVERCOME THE WORLD! If I just let that soak in, God's peace begins to wash over me. No matter what your trial is, no matter how painful it may be, peace is still ours from the One who has overcome all that the enemy tries to dish out. The ending has already been written. Jesus wins and as Believers, we in turn win as a result of Jesus' victory. And that means that Satan loses ... big time! And that visual allows me to take a deep breath and exhale. So today, whatever battle you are in, you can find peace in the midst of the storm by doing exactly what Jesus instructed us to do ... trust Him and take courage because He has overcome the world. If we take that promise to heart, our hearts will survive the ugliness that this world can throw our way because Jesus is with us.

Lord, there is a lot of ugliness in this world. You know because You experienced it, too. Thank You for the reminder that we can have courage and peace because You have overcome the world. Amen.

106...CALL IN THE CAVALRY

Good morning! My sister and I were talking about a situation we were dealing with and she said that it was time to bring in the "Calvary," which of course was a slip of the tongue. Google gave me the definitions of the word she meant to say, "cavalry" and of the word she used "Calvary."

Calvary-A hill near Jerusalem on which Jesus was crucified

cavalry-soldiers who fought on horseback

Her slip of the tongue was actually a great analogy. Because Jesus died on the cross at Calvary, He has become the greatest Soldier for us, as He wants to fight our battles. Exodus 14:14 says, "The Lord will fight for you while you keep silent."

What do you do when people verbally attack or speak untruths about you? Our flesh wants to lash back. You know, fighting fire with fire. We feel like we have to defend ourselves. But that never turns out good. The reason for that is because God says that He wants to fight our battles for us. But there is a caveat. We are told to keep silent. Don't respond, just stay quiet, even when they come back to try to soften their hurtful words. The thing about words is that once they're spoken, you can't take them back. Words are powerful and can have a lingering effect, either positively or negatively. We can't control the words and actions of others. What we can control are our responses. And those responses are what God will hold us accountable for. I know other's words can be painful but try to remember that our battle isn't against flesh and blood (aka people) as Ephesians 6:12 tells us. Those with sharp tongues are just allowing Satan to use them as a weapon to harm others with their words, but what Satan meant for evil, God uses for His good.

Lord, when negative words are thrown our way, help us to just step back and call in Jesus to fight the battle for us. Amen.

107...GREAT ANTICIPATION

Good morning! Anticipation is something we all experience in our day-to-day lives. My girlfriend was just blessed with her first grandson. It was so much fun watching her wait with great anticipation for his arrival. She was bubbling over with excitement. But some things we anticipate are not so good. One of my sweet, sweet girlfriends was recently waiting to find out what cancer treatments the doctor wanted her to take. That kind of anticipation can keep you awake at night if you don't give it all over to the Lord, which is exactly what my girlfriend has done. Whether you're waiting for something good or maybe something not so good, in my mind, there are two parts to anticipation. The first part is that something else has to happen first. For the examples above, it took nine months for my girlfriend to get her grandbaby. And for my cancer friend, she had to go through all the testing and surgeries before the treatment could come. So once you go through part one, part two can happen. That grandbaby is born, and the treatments begin to restore her health.

One thing that I am anticipating more than anything else in my life is seeing Jesus face-to-face. Whether that be if He has come back for His children here on earth or that I have died and entered eternity in heaven with Him that way. But before either of those part two events can happen, Part One must happen. And that's the part that we are all living in today. John 14:6 tells us how we can be assured that we will be with Jesus for all eternity. In Jesus' own words He said, "I am the way, and the truth, and the life; no one comes to the Father but through Me." So how then do we come to the Father through Jesus? Romans 10:9 gives us that answer. It says that "...if you confess with your mouth Jesus as Lord, and believe in your heart that God raised Him from the dead, you will be saved." It's just that simple to ensure yourself an eternity spent with the Lord Almighty in the place of great anticipation ... Heaven.

Lord, please help those that need to still need to accept Your gift of salvation by asking You to be their Lord and Savior. Amen.

108...GIVING THANKS

Good morning! A couple of nights ago, my friend and I were having dinner celebrating some good news. It was fun because we looked back over all of the things that had to transpire before the good news was able to be given.

You know, it's easy to be thankful when things are going smoothly in our life. Things like when your family is healthy and happy, or when there's enough money in your bank account, or when you get that job promotion. It's easy to give thanks when the blessings are so obvious, like when you find out that you are finally pregnant and will be having a bundle of joy to take care of in a few months, or when someone you've been praying for finally accepts Jesus Christ as their Lord and Savior.

But do you give thanks to the Lord when things are not going smoothly? You know, times when there are rough waters within your family, or you can't pay all your bills this month. How about really difficult times like when the doctor says there's nothing else they can do to help your loved one get better? And can you give thanks during those times when you feel like your world has come crashing down on you? 1 Thessalonians 5:18 gives us God's answer to those questions. "In everything give thanks; for this is God's will for you in Christ Jesus." Giving thanks for the good is easy. Giving thanks for the tough times is easy, too. (You thought I was going to say hard, right?) Giving thanks during tough times has lots of positive benefits for us. First, it allows us to hand our problems over to the Lord, thus, lightening our load by placing the problem in His very capable hands. It gives us the opportunity to acknowledge God's sovereignty, which gives us a clearer path to learn whatever God is wanting to teach us through the trials. I don't know all the details of your life, but from my experiences, thanking God for the troubling times will help give us the peace that we all so desperately need during life's valleys.

Lord, help us to thank You for all things ... good and bad. Amen.

109...IT'S NOT JUST LEMONADE

Good morning! Last week after I had finished my cardio rehab session at the hospital, I treated myself to a lemonade from Panera Bread. There were several cars in line at the drive thru so I waited patiently for my turn. When I pulled up to the window to get my lemonade, the lady told me that there was no charge because the person in the drive thru ahead of me had paid for it. That employee was grinning from ear to ear and my smile soon matched hers. Now I know it was only a glass of lemonade, but that kindness from a total stranger touched at least two people's hearts that day.

As I was thinking about that blessing this morning, two thoughts struck my mind. The first one was that I'm still thinking about that stranger's kindness and the smile from last week returned to my face once again this morning. The second thought I'm having is about the impact that one act of kindness can have. You know, our main job here on earth is to share the gospel of Jesus Christ. We are to love others like Jesus loves us. Each act of kindness will help to draw others to the Lord.

Hebrews 13:16 tells us to "not neglect doing good and sharing, for with such sacrifices God is pleased." From time to time in my life I've heard others say that they wanted to make a difference in this world. They were wanting to have a big platform so they could impact many. Very few of us are given that big platform but we all can make an impact in this world by daily reaching out to others by spreading kindness to those we encounter. It's the little things we do that can make a big difference in someone's life. As Believers, we have been so blessed through the love and sacrifice of Jesus. It should be a natural thing for us to extend that love to others in a multitude of ways. So, as we go through our day, here's to spreading kindness as an overflowing of the joy we have in our hearts thanks to Jesus.

Lord, help us to be an extension of Your love to others. Amen.

110...BUILDING BRIDGES

Good morning! As we go through this life, there are many decisions that are "optional." And most of those optional decisions don't have much of an impact on our lives. Decisions like what restaurant you go to for lunch, or whether to take an umbrella with you to work if there is a chance of rain. We make dozens of those kind of optional decisions in the course of a day. But there are some decisions that we think are optional but they really aren't. Forgiveness is one of those decisions. When someone hurts you, even if they hurt you to the core of your heart, we are commanded to forgive them. We find out why in Jesus' own words in Matthew 6:14-15:

"For if you forgive others for their transgressions, your heavenly Father will also forgive you. But if you do not forgive others, then your Father will not forgive your transgressions."

I love it when the Lord is crystal clear with His instructions for us! Our flesh naturally wants to lash right back when others hurt us and Satan will do his best to keep reminding you of the wrong done to you by bringing it back up time after time. It's his very predictable manner to stir the pot, as the old saying goes. But once you forgive your offender, and tell Satan to go back to hell where he belongs, God will start mending your heart as only He can. Choosing to not forgive others only creates a wall between you and that person and you and God. If God was willing to send His only Son to the cross to die in our place for the forgiveness of our sins, then how could we not forgive others? As my pastor said on Sunday, we are called not to build walls but to build bridges. So as you're reading this morning devotion, is there anyone that comes to your mind that you still haven't forgiven? The Good News about forgiveness is that we don't have to do it alone. Like everything else in life, the Lord will equip us to do everything He asks us to do, and forgiving others is something that He will help us do when our hearts are willing. So, here's to letting God be our engineer as we build those bridges.

Heavenly Father, with Your help we can do everything, including forgiving others. Amen.

111...SOME OF HEAVEN ON EARTH

Good morning! If April showers do indeed bring May flowers, then we're going to have an abundance of flowers come next month based on all the rain that we've been having. Although the ground needs the moisture, while it's raining, we don't always appreciate what the rain will produce later for us. Once the rain stops and the sun begins to shine, things are going to get really green around here.

I don't think we always appreciate how the Son, Jesus, shines in our lives all the time either. When things are going smoothly in our lives, we tend to forget the source of that peaceful life. But when things aren't running smoothly, it's just like the rain. We gripe and complain about things while they're happening and often wonder why God is allowing it to happen. But when the rain passes, I think we too often forget to praise the God who brought us through the storm.

Psalm 34:1-3 says,

> *I will bless the Lord at all times; His praise shall continually be in my mouth. My soul will make its boast in the Lord; the humble will hear it and rejoice. O magnify the Lord with me, and let us exalt His name together.*

This verse reminds me of what Heaven will be like. Everything that has breath will praise the Lord. Together, we will praise His name. But we don't have to wait until we get to Heaven to praise Him together. What can you praise God for right now? If you woke up and were breathing this morning, that's a good place to start. My prayer for us is that we would make a conscience effort to continually have the Lord's praises on our lips and experience some Heaven here on earth.

Lord, forgive us for not always being thankful for all that You have done in our lives. Help us praise You throughout our days. Amen.

112...KEEPING YOUR BALANCE

Good morning! Several times a week I'm at the hospital doing cardio rehab. They don't want to let you leave after your session until your heart rate is within 10 points from what it was when you came in. The other day as I was sitting in the recliner waiting for my heart rate to come down, they told me to close my eyes and picture myself relaxing on a beach somewhere. Even though we tried to change my focus, it didn't help anything. My heart rate just wasn't willing to come down that day. As they well know, my heart has a mind of its own.

In a recent *Jesus Calling* devotion, it explained how a spinning ballerina has to keep her eyes focused on one given point. If she doesn't do that, she will lose her balance. Our minds focus on literally hundreds of things each day. So many things require our attention. But in order to live the successful life the Lord wants us to live, our focus has to always return to Him. Without that focus, we can lose our way. Hebrews 12:2 says that we are to fix "our eyes on Jesus, the author and perfecter of faith, who for the joy set before Him endured the cross, despising the shame, and has sat down at the right hand of the throne of God."

Sometimes we can be as stubborn as my heart is, wanting to do things our own way and on our timetable instead of God's. Life is constantly changing around us and if we don't keep our focus on God, we can spin out of control. But the good news is that focusing on the Lord allows our stubborn minds to quit thinking about our problems and also allows us to get out of God's way as He handles our issues in His perfect timing. So, here's to focusing in on what's important.

Heavenly Father, there is so much that distracts us in the course of our day. Our balance is often thrown off because we lose our focus on You. Holy Spirit, please help us regain our focus through listening to Your promptings. Amen.

113...FOOTPRINTS

Good morning! Have you ever noticed that the world views things so differently than how God sees them? Take weaknesses for an example. In our world any weakness is seen as, well, a weakness. Instead the things that are valued as our strengths are our health and physical fitness, and our independence and self-sufficiency. But God views weakness in a totally different light. Our determination and will power can only take us so far in life. Have you ever given something all you had but still fell short, sometimes way short? It's when we've exhausted all our own energy that God carries us through. There is a familiar poem called *Footprints in the Sand*. In this poem, it talks about how a man had a dream that he was walking on the beach with the Lord. As they walked, scenes of his life flashed in the sky. During those times he saw two sets of footprints in the sand. But when there were great struggles in his life and those scenes flashed in the sky, he only saw one set of footprints. The poem explains that the reason for only one set of footprints in the sand was because during those challenging periods of life, God was carrying him.

In 2 Corinthians 12:7-10, Paul talks about his weakness. He said that he was given a thorn in his flesh to keep him from being prideful and exulting himself. He asked God three times to remove that thorn and each time the Lord said that His grace was sufficient, for His power was perfected in weakness. In verse 10, we see Paul's response. "Therefore I am well content with weaknesses, with insults, with distresses, with persecutions, with difficulties, for Christ's sake; for when I am weak, then I am strong." So how many sets of footprints in the sand would you see right now? If you answered, two sets of footprints, you are blessed. But if at this time of pain and suffering, you only see one set of footprints in the sand, you are truly blessed because that means that you, being a child of God, are being cared for and carried by the King of Kings and the LORD of Lords.

Lord, thank you for all the times You carry me in this life. Amen.

114...SAYING YES

Good morning! Yesterday was such a cool day. I woke up to a text message that one of my dear friend's son was going to be baptized last night. He is only 8 years old and already understands that he is in need of a Savior. His baptism is an outward statement that he has accepted the gift of salvation.

As I was thinking about the decision that my friend's son made, I was thinking about why Jesus was called the Lamb of God. Back in biblical times, the Israelites' law said that they needed a blood offering as an atonement for sin. Leviticus 17:11 says, "For the life of the flesh is in the blood, and I have given it to you on the altar to make atonement for your souls; for it is the blood by reason of the life that makes atonement." So, the Israelites would offer up an unblemished animal, often a lamb, to God to be their atonement for their sins. The blood from the animal provided only a temporary covering of their sins. In contrast, when Jesus died on the cross for us, He became the perfect and ultimate sacrifice for our sins. No further sacrifices would have to be brought to the altar. Jesus, the perfect Lamb, by His shed blood on the cross, would forever cover the sins of those who called Him the Lamb of God for all eternity. As the sacrificial Lamb, Jesus exchanged His life for ours. He paid the price for what we owed because of our sins. He became the Perfect atonement for our sin debt.

You know how Jesus is our perfect example for how we should live out our lives? John 15:13 says, "Greater love has no one than this, that one lay down his life for his friends." Jesus did exactly this on Calvary. The only question we must all answer is the one that my friend's son answered yesterday. Have you accepted Jesus' atonement for your sins, and being adopted into the family of God, does Jesus call you friend? A question is definitely worth answering. Your answer will impact the rest of your life, for all eternity. Praying you say "yes."

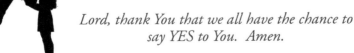

Lord, thank You that we all have the chance to say YES to You. Amen.

115...NO IDOLS

Good morning! We've all heard the phrase, "You can't have it both ways." We can all see this phrase play out on a daily basis. Examples like when you proclaim to be madly in love with your spouse while you're having an affair. Or when you brag about how good of an employee you are while at the same time you are stealing from the owner.

While those examples seem extreme, I have one more example that takes the cake. It's when you say Jesus is Your Lord and Savior while at the same time you are serving an idol. Exodus 20:3-6 says,

> *"You shall have no other gods before me. You shall not make for yourself an idol, or any likeness of what is in heaven above or on the earth beneath or in the water under the earth. You shall not worship them or serve them; for I, the Lord your God, am a jealous God, visiting the iniquity of the fathers on the children, on the third and the fourth generations of those who hate me, but showing lovingkindness to thousands, to those who love me and keep My commandments."*

In the Old Testament days, idols were easier to identify. They were actually something you could see, like golden calves or Baal. Today our idols are not so obvious but still as destructive. People worship themselves, others like a star athlete, money, power, control, and status to name a few. But just like in the Old Testament days, worshipping these things is never satisfying. They're never enough. That's why you have to put more energy and invested more time in trying to satisfy yourself with these idols. If we would just put down the idols of this world and pick up everything that Jesus has to offer, we would be satisfied like no other. So, what idols are you hanging on to today? Whatever they are, they won't provide you with what you're looking for. Only Jesus can do that. Praying today is the day we toss our idols out the window and begin only serving and worshipping the Lord.

Lord, please show us any idols that we need to get rid of. Amen.

116...DRAW NEAR TO GOD

Good morning! Are you blessed with amazing family and friends? I know I am and those relationships mean the world to me. I was thinking last night about what it takes to maintain those relationships. The same common thread ran through my answers for each one of them. It takes time. A relationship isn't going to develop or stay strong if you're not willing to put the time in. It should be a joy to spend time with them, pray for them, and be involved in their lives. As I began reflecting about the most important relationship of my life, my relationship with the Lord, I realized that the same truth holds true in maintaining a relationship with God as it does with my other family and friends. James 4:8 says, "Draw near to God and He will draw near to you." Drawing near to God takes time. It requires us to stop everything we're doing and make time to hear from God.

Just like the story of Mary and Martha in Luke 10:38-42, Mary was sitting at Jesus' feet listening to Him but Martha was complaining to Jesus that Mary was not helping her with the preparations. And Jesus' reply to Martha is found in verses 41-42. "Martha, Martha, you are worried and bothered about so many things; but only one thing is necessary, for Mary has chosen the good part, which shall not be taken away from her." Sound familiar? How many times in the course of the day do we not hear God because we are so distracted with things that don't really matter. We worry and fret and sometimes just come totally unglued over stuff that really just doesn't matter. The Lord wants us to stop worrying, and start listening intently for His voice. The Lord speaks softly so if our thoughts are being cluttered with other voices or noise, we aren't going to hear Him. If we could only silence the noise in our heads like we can our phones, we'd have a much better chance of hearing the Lord speak. That's where the Holy Spirit comes in. Asking Him to silence the noise in our heads so we can just focus on God before we sit quietly before the Lord is always a beneficial move.

Lord, help us to be more like Mary and less like Martha. Amen.

117...TURN OFF THE FAUCET

Good morning! It's that time of year where families are taking vacations. Some drive to their destination and others fly the friendly skies to get to where they are going. Either way you travel, every successful trip needs to start with a full tank. A full tank of fuel. A full tank of food. And most importantly, a full tank of Jesus. Sometimes our tanks get depleted because of the drama that often comes with life. In case you don't already know this, none of us are perfect. But some people have no tolerance for others. When things don't go exactly as they think they should, they tend to not be nice. But I was listening to a friend of mine at church yesterday and I can't shake what he said. Everything we say, either orally or in a written format, is a choice. So, when people have unkind things to say about you, you have a choice on how you're going to respond. My friend said that we were like a faucet which we can either choose to turn on or turn off. God tells us the best thing that we can do when others attack us, is to just stand. This is how it is said in Ephesians 6:10-11. "Finally, be strong in the Lord and in the strength of His might. Put on the full armor of God, so that you will be able to stand firm against the schemes of the devil." And make no mistake about it, it is the enemy who shoots those fiery arrows at us. He's just using people to carry out his schemes.

Life isn't going to always be like a vacation. Things aren't going to always be smooth sailing. We shouldn't be too surprised when the enemy tries his best to attack us. That's just what life here in a sinful, fallen world is like. But one day, everything will be different for Believers when we move from here to Paradise and live for all eternity with our Lord and Savior in Heaven where the enemy can't live. My prayer for us all is that we would indeed be that faucet my friend spoke about and turn off the drama and turn on God's strength and just silently stand so our Heavenly Father can fight the battles for us. May we resist the desire of the flesh to fire back the arrows thrown at us, and instead, go about doing the things God has called us to do.

Lord, help us to be strong enough to turn off the faucet. Amen.

118...TWO LINES, ONE CHOICE

Good morning! I am still praising God this morning for the safe rescue of the 12 boys and their coach from the cave in Thailand they were stranded in. The Lord brought many countries together for one common goal. And because of their efforts, thirteen families are rejoicing that their loved one is alive. But one of the divers on Day 1 of the rescue died as he tried to save those boys. Our hearts go out to his family and friends for their loss. I was praying for those he loved when I read John 15:12-15:

> *"This is My commandment, that you love one another, just as I have loved you. Greater love has no one than this, that one lay down his life for his friends. You are my friends if you do what I command you. No longer do I call you slaves, for the slave does not know what the master is doing; but I have called you friends, for all things that I have heard from My Father I have made known to you."*

We might not ever have to lay our lives down for another like this diver did, but our hearts should be ready to do just that. Being ready to do that means we also have to be ready to stand before the Lord on Judgement Day. Every person in this universe will be held accountable by God for the choices and actions of our lives. There will be two judgments ... one for those who had accepted Jesus as their Lord and Savior, and one for those that didn't accept Jesus. For Believers, we will be judged on what we did with our life here on earth. Those things will be judged by God to see if any of them deserve rewards in heaven. And the second judgment that Revelation 20 calls the Great White Throne judgment, will be based on whether their names will be found in the Book of Life. Since they did not accept Jesus as their Lord and Savior while they were here on earth, their names will not be found in that book and the lake of fire will be their forever home. The Good News is that we can choose which judgment line we will stand in. And just like

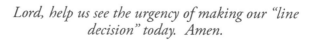 we know from the diver's death, there's no guarantee for tomorrow. Is time running out for you to make your decision?

Lord, help us see the urgency of making our "line decision" today. Amen.

119...SMILING FROM THE INSIDE OUT

Good morning! Blessings come in all sorts of shapes and sizes and I have received some of the biggest blessings recently. God has shown Himself mightily in my life and I am so thankful for all He's done. But I don't want to overlook all the smaller blessings that are happening, too. Blessings like my heart friend sending me an angel emoji after he reads my morning texts. It warms my heart every day and makes me smile from the inside out. And isn't it a sweet blessing when people really listen to you? After the auction was over on Sunday, a friend made and brought me a strawberry-rhubarb pie. My sister, brother in-law and I had lunch at her restaurant two days before the auction at my home. She heard us talking about the pies she had displayed. That conversation brought up a childhood memory of my mom making the best ever strawberry-rhubarb pie. So, my friend brought me comfort food knowing I could use a pick-me-up after the auction. Even though that pie is gone now, that small blessing will forever be etched on my heart. We can get so busy in our day-to-day lives that we don't make time to listen to others or do those small blessings that means so much.

James 1:17 says, "Every good thing given and every perfect gift is from above, coming down from the Father of lights, with whom there is no variation or shifting shadow." When we bless others through any size of a blessing, big or small, we are being an extension of the Lord's love coming down from above.   I don't know what's on your schedule for today, but I know I want to find a way to bless someone today. With that being my heart's desire, I am confident that the Lord will guide me and give me that opportunity to be a blessing to someone. So, here's to helping others smile from the inside out.

Heavenly Father, thank You for giving us
opportunities to be extensions of Your love.
Amen.

120...MOVE TO THE KINGDOM OF LIGHT

Good morning! Today is a bitter-sweet day for me ... it's Alan's birthday. Oh, how I miss that man! I know many of you miss him terribly, too. My tears quit flowing when I stop and try to imagine what a celebration he is experiencing everyday living in Paradise ... living in the Kingdom of light. In Acts 26:18, Jesus is telling Saul what He wanted him to do. He told Saul to get up and go out in order for others to "open their eyes so that they may turn from darkness to light and from the dominion of Satan to God, that they may receive forgiveness of sins and an inheritance among those who have been sanctified by faith in Me." So, this world, including all those who haven't yet put their faith in Jesus, is living under the rule of Satan, the Kingdom of Darkness. That thought should cause us to take notice.

But just like Alan knew, you don't have to stay in the Kingdom of Darkness. Colossians 1:12-14 says,

> *"Giving thanks to the Father, who has qualified us to share in the inheritance of the saints in Light. For He rescued us from the domain of darkness, and transferred us to the kingdom of His beloved Son, in whom we have redemption, the forgiveness of sins."*

Once you accept the gift of salvation and ask Jesus to forgive you of your sins, you have moved from the Kingdom of Darkness into the Kingdom of Light. And just like Alan, Heaven will be your forever home!

So, until God calls us home, like He did Alan over two years ago, we have a very specific job to do. We are to be the witnesses of Jesus, sharing with others who He is and what He has done for us. One of these days as Believers, we will experience what our birthdays will be like in heaven. But until then, we can thank God that He takes what we think are bitter-sweet days and reminds us just how sweet they really are.

Lord, thank You for the assurance that You have given us through the shed blood of Jesus. There is peace in knowing where we and our loved ones will spend eternity as Believers. Amen.

121...PAINTING A GOOD EXAMPLE

Good morning! There is nothing I enjoy more in this life than seeing God move in the lives of those I love. I'm not just talking about when they come to Jesus and salvation is theirs, which is the most important decision of their life, but the day-to-day things. For example, one of my girlfriends is undergoing cancer treatments which we can all agree is bad, but the Lord is blessing her socks off as she goes through this trial. If she hadn't had to quit the job she was doing because of her cancer, she might not ever have fully developed one of her God-given talents, painting. Because of having time to paint between treatments, she has blessed so many people through the memories she has captured for them through the canvases she paints. And it's showing everyone how God provides for His children, on so many levels.

One of the Psalms that I love is Psalm 34:8. "Oh taste and see that the Lord is good; how blessed is the man [or woman] who takes refuge in Him." In order to see just how good our God is, you have to have your eyes wide open and make the decision to look for God's goodness. In everything in life, we have a choice. My girlfriend could choose to focus on the cancer or she could choose to focus on the talent that God has given her. She has the choice of looking at the positive or the negative, just like the rest of us do for every situation that we encounter. She made the decision we all should make. She chose to look at the positive side of things. Those around her are all witnessing how God has taken something bad, cancer, and has made good come from it, just like He promises He'll do in Romans 8:28. "And we know that God causes all things to work together for good to those who love God, to those who are called according to His purpose." So, my prayer for all of us is for our eyes to be opened so we can clearly see all the ways God is showing His goodness in our everyday moments.

Lord, we thank You for keeping Your promise that You will take the bad and make something good out of it for those that love You and You've painted quite a picture with this example. Amen.

122...HE'S WORKING

Good morning! Yesterday I wrote about looking for God's goodness in our day-to-day lives. I told you about how through my girlfriend's cancer, God was blessing so many through the paintings that she now had time to do between treatments. It's beautiful to see God orchestrating so many blessings during this time in her life. But this morning, after learning about another girlfriend's brother who just found out he has level 4 glioblastoma, I began thinking about the reasons that God allows trials in our lives and was taken to a verse found in Luke. Luke 1:79 says, "To shine upon those who sit in darkness and the shadow of death, to guide our feet into the way of peace." Wouldn't it be easier to deal with hard times if we knew in advance how God was going to use those difficult times to bless us and others as He turns bad into good? It most definitely would be easier, but that doesn't require any faith. One reason He allows difficult times is to increase our faith in Him and conform us to be more Christ-like.

Now back to the verse in Luke I referenced earlier. Our trials are not just for us. They also teach and encourage others as they see us persevere through the hard times with the Lord's help. As we carry on with life during our hardships, those who are sitting in darkness because they don't know our Lord and Savior, see His light shine in our lives. The ultimate goal is for them to come to the realization that they need the same Jesus that is carrying us through the hard times. Wouldn't it make our trials easier to bear knowing that our momentary suffering, compared to eternity, could help someone come to a saving relationship with the Lord and guarantee their place in heaven? We have to remember that nothing in our life is random or meaningless. God uses our pain and suffering to make us more like Jesus and to help others on their path with the Lord. So, whatever your hardship is, remember that God has a purpose for you enduring the trial and that He is right there in the middle of it working out His perfect plan for your life and all those who love Him.

Lord, help us to see Your hand at work during tough times. Amen.

123...BEING INTENTIONAL

Good morning! Do you ever just wish you could reach up and grab your thought and hold on to it so you could give it the time and attention it needs? With all the changes in my life lately, I have found myself having so many thoughts running through my mind and I just want to hang on to that one thought and then when I try to get it, it's gone. Poof! And it disappears. And then sometime later that day or night, I'll remember what that thought was but it's usually too late for that thought to be useful. When my thoughts are bouncing around in my mind, it's kind of like throwing popcorn up in the wind and watching it blow everywhere.

It's not just my day-to-day thoughts that this happens to, it also happens when I'm praying. To say it's frustrating is an understatement! I want to be intentional when I'm talking to the Lord, giving Him my everything but that doesn't always happen. I don't want to be "driven and tossed by the wind" as James 1:6 says.

Our minds are powerful, but we need to control our minds instead of letting them control us. What do we do to lasso our thoughts when we try to talk with God? For me, I'm finding that if I close my eyes and take a deep breath, I am able to recite Psalm 46:10 over and over until my mind quiets down. "Be still and know that I am God." This is a command, not a suggestion...a command that I have to work on every day. My desire is to be able to capture my thoughts and run them through God's filters, leaving only the productive ones behind in my mind. I guess you could say that I'm still a work in progress where this is concerned. My prayer is that I'd be purposeful in my thoughts and actions, and I pray the same for you.

Lord, when we talk, I want to give You my full attention but that doesn't always work. Thank You for understanding when my thoughts get interrupted and for helping me return my focus to You. Amen.

124...THE BEST PATH

Good morning! I was given some goals at my cardio rehab last week. Let's just say it was a good thing I was sitting down when they told me these goals. At that moment, I thought that there was no way possible that those goals would ever be met. I must've had a look on my face that was matching my thoughts because they told me that this is a goal that we're working towards and that it's not going happen overnight but it's our goal. There are a couple of problems with the way I was looking at these new goals. First of all, all I can see is the present. From my current perspective, I'm not seeing what the nurses are seeing for me. Even though the rehab nurses can see progress, it's often hard for me to see it as gradual as it is. Second, they've seen many other patients in cardio rehab and as a result, they have confidence that I will reach the goals eventually. I just have to trust that they are taking me down the right path to help my heart get stronger.

I know I've done the same thing in my walk with the Lord. A situation arises and I look at those circumstances from my limited perspective. I see it from my "here and now" eyes instead of from God's all-knowing eyes. Even though we can't see what all God is doing, doesn't mean we can't trust Him. Thinking about this reminded me of my favorite verse in the Bible, Proverbs 3:5-6. "Trust in the Lord with all your heart and do not lean on your own understanding. In all your ways acknowledge Him, and He will make your paths straight." I know that I can trust the Lord one hundred percent to lead me down the right path, and that helps my faith in Him grow stronger. I know He sees and knows all and that He is in total control of every aspect of my life. But sometimes I just need a reminder and He is gracious enough to provide me with those reminders through His Word, through other Believers, and through my own past experiences where He has shown Himself mightily in my life. So, could you use a reminder today, too?

Lord, thank You for leading us down the best path for our lives, the one where You are right there beside us. Amen.

125...SERVING OTHERS

Good morning! What character traits do you value in others? Are ambition and self-promotion, doing what it takes to get ahead in this life, two of the traits that you think are important? If so, a lot of people would agree with you. Unfortunately our culture is becoming very me-oriented. You know, everything is about me, myself and I. But none of these traits are things that God deems as important. When God sent His only Son to us, He gave us the perfect example of the character traits that we should strive for. Humility was one of those traits. As Christians, we need to follow the example that Jesus showed us. Christ did not come to be served but to serve, so we should be about serving others as well. Philippians 2:3 says, "Do nothing from selfish or empty conceit, but with humility of mind regard one another as more important than yourselves."

So what does "regard one another as more important than yourself" look like? There are many ways to do this but I believe one of the best ways to serve others is by giving them your time. I know everyone has busy schedules but for me, nothing says better that "I love you," "I care about you," or "You are important to me," than when others give me their time. It doesn't have to be anything major. It could just be simply taking a couple minutes to text or call a friend. Or it can be like what my girlfriend did yesterday. She knew that yesterday was my wedding anniversary and that I would be missing Alan, so a week ago she asked if she could have dinner with me and just hang out. I know she has a lot of things to do with her school ending their school year today, but she still gave me her time. That's what it means to serve one another in love. So how are you doing in the service department? If it doesn't come easily for you to put others first, that just means you are following your natural tendencies to focus on yourself. To live a life of humility like Jesus did requires the help of the Holy Spirit. He's ready to help you. All you have to do is ask.

Holy Spirit, thank You for always being there to help us. Amen.

126...HERE I AM, SEND ME

Good morning! I was listening to the birds at my new house again this morning. Until yesterday, all I had seen around my new home were the birds that just cause trouble, the blackbirds. They make a mess everyplace they go, and in the evening they gather all along the electric line that runs across my backyard and make some terrible noises. These birds remind me of life. If you turn on the news and listen to the broadcast, chances are you're going to hear one bad thing after another. And if the bad things weren't terrible enough, they interview people to make everything sound worse than it already was. It's almost as though we thrive on the bad. Believe it or not, they actually have to set aside a special segment just to bring some good news. They act like it's a rare thing to have anything good to report, suggesting that there's just not much good in this world. But that's hogwash!

Yes, there is evil in this world, and we are seeing a lot of it. But as God's children, we are the good of this world and we need to spread His goodness. In Isaiah 6:8 the Lord asked Isaiah whom He should send to spread the gospel and Isaiah's response was, "Here am I. Send me!" That should be all of our answers to God's call for us to spread the gospel to all parts of this hurting world. True, we may not be able to go to the remote parts of this world, but we can go out into our communities and shine Jesus' light to those that we see. It's time for all Believers to rise up and take a stand for our Lord. Even though the evil is out there, like the blackbirds lining up on the power lines, we can still be the beauty because we carry with us the Hope, and the answer to all the hurting and desperate people out there. What this world needs is a lot more of Jesus. But the choice is ours. We can be like the blackbirds, loud and unruly offering nothing but a mess, or we can bring God's love and His message of hope to all we meet. So my prayer for all of us is that we will say, "Yes Lord, here I am, send me!!"

Lord, help us bring Your message of hope to this world. Amen.

127...THE BEST FRIEND

Good morning! A couple of days ago I had the opportunity to show one of my friends my new house. She is such a sweetheart and true to her nature, she brought me a little housewarming gift. The saying on the towel she gave me said, "Good friends are like stars, you don't always see them, but you know they're always there." I love that quote and it is such a good reminder for me that my good friends are always there for me through all the seasons of my life. I think there are three types of friends in this world. The one who is your friend for what they can get from you and when they feel they can't get any more from you, they move on. They are a "good season" type of friend. As long as things are happy go lucky, they are there for you. But if a problem comes up, they are outta here! I prefer to call these types of friends just merely acquaintances. The second type of friend is much more than a "fair weather" friend. They are there for the good times and the bad. They celebrate the joys in your life, no matter how big or small they are. And when hardship comes, they dig their heels in with you and they help you fight the battle until the victory is won. They stick to you like peanut butter on bread. You consider them as some of your greatest blessings in life.

But the best friend is the third type of friend. We find out why there is only one Friend in this category in Hebrews 13:5. Jesus Himself said, "I will never desert you, nor will I ever forsake you." as good as your dearest friends are, they're only human. Being human, they can't be with you 24/7. Jesus is the only One who can be with you for every moment in your life. But sometimes we take that blessing for granted. He is always there but we don't always see Him or even acknowledge Him. So, my prayer for all of us today is that we will cherish the Lord as our greatest blessing and that we will focus on trying to see Him continuously through every moment of our lives.

Lord, again, we say thank You for being our constant companion and friend. Thank You for not leaving our side. Amen.

127

128...HE'LL CARRY THEM

Good morning! What do you do when bad news comes knocking at your door? Being human, I think we all react in some form of disbelief, which is only normal. But after that initial shock is over, how do we handle it? Do we carry it with us like a dark cloud in a thunderstorm? Does it consume our every thought? Or do we allow it to completely stop us in our tracks?

The Lord doesn't want us to be held hostage by troubling times or bad news. 1 Peter 5:7 tells us to cast all of our anxiety on the Lord because He cares for us. And I love what Psalm 55:22 says. "Cast your burden upon the Lord and He will sustain you; He will never allow the righteous to be shaken." It's amazing how the weight of a problem can be lifted off of our shoulders when we make the decision to just give our problems over to the Lord. He has big shoulders and really wants us to transfer the weight of our problems to Him. The problems that can paralyze us can easily be handled by the Lord.

If this is speaking to you this morning, like it spoke to me, I'd like to propose a challenge for us. We are starting the Memorial Day weekend today. If you have problems and troubles that are weighing heavily on you, give them over to the Lord today, *right now*. But here's the catch. Leave the problems with Him all weekend. Don't pick them back up later today or tomorrow. When the enemy starts speaking lies to you that God needs your help with handling them or that you could handle them better, tell the enemy to take a hike. Let God carry the problems for you and just see how much more you can enjoy this long weekend with family and friends. I promise that you will notice a huge difference. I did it myself this morning and I already feel better. Praying you are up to the challenge.

Lord, help us to quit listening to the lies of the enemy and believe You when You say that You've got this, regardless of what the problem is. Thank You, Lord, for carrying them for us. Amen.

129...PRAY IT

Good morning! When I get to Heaven, one of the people I want to meet is the psalmist David. He poured His heart out to the Lord in the psalms he wrote. As I was reading Psalm 25, God reminded me of some of the reasons we need to pray. I think we all pray when trouble comes knocking on our door or on the door of those we love. Times like when your child or granddaughter is taken to the ER, or when a friend is needing surgery. I think that when these types of situations arise, we have no trouble praying to the Lord. But other times when we need to be praying, we don't run to God first. We try to do it or figure it out ourselves and I have learned that that is not the wisest thing to do. Are you trying to make an important decision? If you seek the Lord, He will instruct you how you should go. He will give you the guidance that you need, if you just pray and ask Him.

The two areas that I should pray about constantly are sometimes the last two that come to mind. Every single day I need to ask for God's forgiveness because I know I have fallen short. Even though I try to be the best I can be, I know I fall way short of the mark. And by falling short of where God would have me be, I know I need His daily cleansing to help be more like Jesus. Psalm 25:19-20 gives me *the* thing I should definitely include in my prayers:

> *"Look upon my enemies, for they are many, and they hate me with violent hatred. Guard my soul and deliver me; do not let me be ashamed, for I take refuge in you."*

God is the only One who can guard our souls and rescue us from all of the attacks that the enemy will throw at us during each day. With that being said, we should pray and ask Him daily for His protection for us over the enemy. If I would only start each day with this prayer for protection over my enemies, what a difference that would make. With that said, I have a question. Have you started your day off by talking with God? If not, maybe this would be a good time to do so.

Lord, thank you for guarding my soul and delivering me from my enemies. Amen.

130...RISE ABOVE

Good morning! On my flight to Texas, we ran into a thunderstorm. The pilot told us it was going to get a bit bumpy so we needed to take our seats and buckle our seat belts again. He was right but it wasn't turbulent very long. But during the storm, as we rose above those heavy black storm clouds, I saw the coolest thing. Did you know that the top of those black, stormy clouds that we see when we are on the ground, aren't black at all? They are white! Pure white.

Those clouds reminded me of life. Sometimes there are storms in our lives and when they hit, we have two choices. We can either stay in the darkness of the storm cloud or raise our eyes beyond the dark portion of the storm, and look to the Light, Jesus. I've done both in my life and what I can tell you is that if you're like our pilot and rise above the darkness and enter into the Light, you will be better able to deal with the storms when they pop up. Jesus said in John 12:46, "I have come as Light into the world, so that everyone who believes in Me will not remain in darkness."

I was pondering what it meant for Jesus to be the Light of this world. John 8:12 says, "I am the Light of the World. Whoever follows me will never walk in darkness but have the light of life." Just as we would light a candle to dispel the darkness in a room, Jesus came to dispel the darkness of sin in our life. Once we have accepted Him as our Lord and Savior, and the darkness is pushed aside, His Light shines for us and through us, showing us how to live the life He has laid out for us.

My prayer for us today is that we would let the clouds remind us to rise up above the storms of life into the safety of God's Light because there is no better place to be!

Jesus, thank You for showing us Your Light,
especially when we are in the middle of a storm.
Help us rise above the storm to You. Amen.

131...ONE WAY TICKET

Good morning! I got home last night from a trip to Texas. On my flight home, we were delayed for 45 minutes on the plane before we were cleared to take off. It got really hot on the plane while we waited. A gentleman commented that it was hotter than Hell on the plane, which of course was an inaccurate statement, but it started me thinking about Heaven and Hell. As we were taking off and beginning our ascent, I was praying for a safe flight. The Lord reminded me that one day I will be meeting Jesus in the air and I won't need an airplane to get me there. We won't be late because they can't fit everyone and their baggage on the plane. Jesus will take all Believers home to our Heavenly Father and we won't be taking any baggage with us!

1 Thessalonians 4:17 says, "Then we who are alive and remain will be caught up together with them in the clouds to meet the Lord in the air, and so we shall always be with the Lord." If you don't have a reservation for that heavenly transport, today would be a great day to fix that issue. In order to secure that one-way ticket to Paradise, all you have to do is accept the gift of salvation through Jesus Christ. You don't have to have all of the answers. You don't have to understand every word from Genesis to Revelation. You don't have to have your life perfectly in order. (By the way, on this side of Heaven, none of these things are going to happen.) God takes misfits, like you and me, right where we are, and covers us with the blood of Christ at the moment we ask Jesus to be our Lord and Savior. After acknowledging that we have a sin debt that we'll never be able to pay, the good Lord does the rest. We don't have to have frequent flyer miles available to redeem for our one-way ticket to Heaven, because once we're a Believer, we have been redeemed by the blood of Jesus Christ. So, if you haven't made your eternal reservation yet, there's no better time than today to do so. And for all of us who are already Believers, here's to thanking God for that eternal ticket that can't be cancelled.

Lord, thank You for our ticket of salvation.
Destination ... Heaven. Amen.

132...EXULT IN THE LORD

Good morning! Have you ever noticed how our "plans" can be instantly changed? One minute you're feeling great, the next minute ... not so much, so you can't go to wherever you planned. One minute you're enjoying a hobby you love, and the next thing you know, you get hurt. One minute you have your finances all in order so you can start saving money and then an emergency comes up and that plan goes out the window. This list of examples could go on and on as we've all dealt with such unplanned disappointments. So, when these changes in your plans occur, how do you handle the disappointment? Do you lose your mind over it or do you start seeking the Lord to see what it is that He would like for you to learn from this unscheduled event?

Our plans may change but the good news is that God's plans don't. Nothing will change His purpose and that's a promise we can rest on. Habakkuk 3:17-18 tells us what we should do when things don't go as planned.

> *Though the fig tree should not blossom and there be no fruit on the vines, though the yield of the olive should fail and the fields produce no food, though the flock should be cut off from the fold and there be no cattle in the stalls, yet I will exult in the Lord, I will rejoice in the God of my salvation.*

Why would we rejoice in the God of our salvation when our circumstances change? Because God keeps His promises and even though I might not like the change being made to my plans, I know that God's plans are far better than any plans I could ever come up with. Change just means something good is coming down the pike. So what disappointments are you dealing with as a result of an unexpected change? Are you going to let that change defeat you or are you going to exalt the Lord, even if it doesn't make sense? Praying that as we deal with changes and disappointments, we will let God guide us along *His* plan for us.

Lord, help us look for Your good that is on the horizon. Amen.

133...LIMITATIONS

Good morning! Isn't knowing our limitations a good thing??? You know how when you get up in the morning and sleepily walk into the kitchen to get that first cup of coffee, tea or hot chocolate? Yesterday morning as I was making my way into the kitchen to get my mug, I realized I was standing *in water!* Upon further investigation, I learned that one of the pipes had come apart underneath my sink sometime during the night and, unfortunately, I ran the dishwasher right before I went to bed. By the way, did you know that a dishwasher uses *lots* of water?!!! OK, back to limitations. What I discovered in this adventure is ... I am *not* a plumber! I've seen other people use that white tape and then screw the pipe back on but I'm not at all confident that my fix will hold. So, as soon as the fans get things dried out in the kitchen, I'll have someone else look at my handiwork.

The same thing is true in life. We often compare ourselves to others in what we see them do. We wonder how they can have it all together when we're really struggling with issues. But what I have learned over the years is that nobody has it all together. On the surface, it might look like they have it all worked out, but if you spent any time with them and got them talking and allowed them to be real, you find out that they have struggles, too.

The only person we need to compare ourselves to is Jesus. True, we will never be like Him as long as we are still walking on this earth, but He is the one that we need to strive to be like. Ephesians 5:1-2 says, "Therefore be imitators of God, as beloved children; and walk in love, just as Christ also loved you and gave Himself up for us, an offering and a sacrifice to God as a fragrant aroma." It all starts with love. If we could only just master that one thing of loving others like Jesus loves them, we would see such a dramatic change in our lives and in the lives around us.

Lord, help us keep our focus on being an imitator of You. Amen.

134...OUR LIFEGUARD

Good morning! My new friend and sister in Christ from Texas sent me what she recently saw on a church marquee. I'll get to that in a minute. While I was in Texas, we had dinner with her and her husband. During our dinner discussions, I learned that they love to sail and that they can actually *live* on their sail boat. I was so intrigued by that fact and began firing questions at them about all the things I instantly became curious about. Their answers and descriptions were so amazing that I almost felt like I was on the boat. Even though I wasn't on the boat, I sure wanted to be!

Isn't enthusiasm contagious? You can sure fire up a room of people with it. Now let me ask you a question. When was the last time you were *really excited* about something? Hopefully you didn't have to think back beyond a day or two to find that answer. Unfortunately, there are so many hurting souls out there who never let themselves get excited about anything. They have built such a wall around themselves to protect them from any more pain and heartache. They seem to fear everything and they are always waiting for "the other shoe to drop," as the saying goes. But we don't have to live in fear. Isaiah 41:10 says, "Do not fear, for I am with you; do not anxiously look about you, for I am your God. I will strengthen you, surely I will help you, surely I will uphold you with My righteous right hand." When we let God be the anchor of our soul, we need not fear. Just like the anchor for the sail boat, God, as our anchor, will hold us safe and sound regardless of how rough the waves that enter our life become.

God sees all, knows all, and controls all, so we truly have nothing to fear. Now back to that church marquee. I love what it said!

"There is nothing to fear when your Lifeguard walks on water."

 It's a saying that needs to be on a T-shirt with an anchor. It would be a powerful reminder to not live in fear.

Jesus, thank You for being our Lifeguard!

135...INTRODUCTIONS

Good morning! I've been thinking about some of the things God has shown me about my recent trip to Texas. During the eight days I was there, I had the privilege to talk to three groups of people. The Lord reminded me of one commonality for each time I spoke ... someone introduced me. They didn't tell the audience everything they knew about me, instead they just gave them a tidbit of information. And when I spoke, I didn't tell those listening my entire story. I told each group a part of my story that went along with what I was asked to speak about.

Those introductions made me think about the introductions that we are all called to make on a daily basis. God wants us to introduce Jesus to those we encounter. When we talk to them, we don't have to tell them everything we know about Jesus and we don't have to tell them our entire story either. We just give them whatever "chapter" that the Holy Spirit prompts us to share. We are all called to plant these seeds of Christ in others. Once these seeds are planted, the Lord will cultivate them, and will bring home the harvest but it all starts with an introduction.

Our job is to help others fall in love and understand their need for the same Jesus that we have as Believers in our lives. No one is exempt from sharing Jesus with others. Matthew 28:19 gives us the Great Commission.

> *"Go therefore and make disciples of all the nations, baptizing them in the name of the Father and the Son and the Holy Spirit, teaching them to observe all that I have commanded you; and lo, I am with you always, even to the end of the age."*

And before the enemy tries to convince you that you don't have anything to share, if you are a Believer, you have a story to tell. Just share how you came to the point where you knew you needed a Savior and what Jesus has done for you. Be courageous and plant that seed and let the Holy Spirit do the rest.

Lord, we know that You equip us for whatever You call us to do. Help us to be courageous and introduce someone to You. Amen.

136...OUT THE WINDOW

Good morning! Let's start today off with a question. How do you trust the Lord? Do you trust Him totally or are you better at keeping a hand on things, you know, just in case? I'm having to answer that question myself this morning. With my morning devotions, there is always a back story. Sometimes I share that with you, sometimes I don't. But today, I'll share the back story because I'm sure some of you are doing the same thing.

Tomorrow is the real estate auction for the place Alan and I called home for some amazing years. I know it's the right thing to sell it but it's a bitter-sweet thing. Alan always told me that if he passed away first to sell our home and go find a cute, little house, knowing I would not be able to maintain the farm. So, I'm good with that aspect of the sale. What I realized this morning, as I was getting really anxious about the sale tomorrow, is that what I'm anxious about is something I should be trusting the Lord for. No one wants good things for me anymore than God does. He knows every need I have and has been supplying me with everything I need. He has taken care of every detail in my life so far so why should I be anxious about tomorrow's sale? Then I realized that rolling those anxious questions around in my mind was the same thing as not trusting God. So, I told Satan to get behind me and take his questions with him! Romans 15:13 says, "Now may the God of hope fill you with all joy and peace as you trust in Him, so that you will abound in hope by the power of the Holy Spirit." Did you see the caveat? As I trust in God then I'll experience joy and peace in my situation. So, when I wasn't feeling the peace I was longing for, I knew I needed a reality check. And the reality was that I was listening to the wrong voice and therefore was extremely anxious. The blessing from God is that He restores our joy and peace when we turn our anxieties over to Him and trust Him to take care of all the details. And because I know God is trustworthy, "Anxiety, you are outta here!"

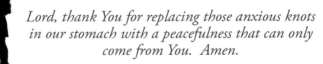

Lord, thank You for replacing those anxious knots in our stomach with a peacefulness that can only come from You. Amen.

137...OUR BEST INTEREST

Good morning! Don't you just love it when people tell you what to do??!! Usually, that answer is a resounding NO! We're human, and we don't always want to be told what to do. But I'll be answering that question much differently in the future because of the sermon my pastor preached yesterday on Jeremiah 33:3. "Call to Me and I will answer you, and I will tell you great and mighty things, which you do not know." In this verse, God is giving us a command, aka, telling us what to do, when He said, "Call to Me." Most people are just being bossy when they try to tell you what to do, but the Lord is commanding us to do this for our good. He says when we call on Him, He will do two things. He will answer our prayer and He will tell us great and mighty things, which we do not know. Wow! When was the last time someone told you what to do and promised you things of this magnitude? When we have trouble show up in our life, our first course of action should be to call out to God. When we do, He will show us what doors we need to go through and which doors we don't need to enter. And because He is a God of integrity, He will answer our prayers in a way that is in our best interest and for His glory.

The second part of that promise is that He will show us great and mighty things, which we do not know. There isn't anyone that I would rather learn from than the Lord. The first part of the verse in Ephesians 3:20 says, "Now to Him who is able to do far more abundantly beyond all that we ask or think..." We can't even imagine all that God is wanting to do in our lives. This is such an amazing truth to hold on to as we deal with the struggles of life. Oh, how I've seen this truth played out in my life time and time again. If you haven't experienced God doing more than you've asked or imagined in your own life yet, follow God's command and call out to Him and watch Him keep His promises.

Lord, thank You for being patient with us as we continue to learn that everything You do and command of us is for our best interest. Amen.

138...IN ITS APPROPRIATE TIME

Good morning! Yesterday, a dear friend of mine had surgery. As we were waiting for her surgery to be finished, I walked across the hall to the hospital's gift shop. Inside the gift shop, I saw this metal sign. Now that I am back home, I sure wish I would have bought it. The sign simply stated Ecclesiastics 3:11. "He has made everything beautiful in its time." I am writing that verse on my heart. God's promise of making everything beautiful in its appropriate time is such a promise of hope. Hope like healing from a surgery ... at it's appropriate time, restoring broken relationships ... at its appropriate time, or sorrow turning into joy ... at its appropriate time.

As we go through life, there are going to be plenty of ugly times. There is just so much ugliness out there and none of us are immune to it, and unfortunately, there isn't any way to escape it either. But, if during those ugly times, we believed that God would keep His promise of eventually turning the ugly into something beautiful, wouldn't it be easier to cope with the ugliness? While I was thinking about this, I caught myself trying to orchestrate what God's beauty would look like. I realized that it is as crazy as trying to put God in a box. God is the Creator of all and He has every resource at His disposal so why would we try to limit what God's beauty is? His beauty is so much more than what we can fathom.

When is the last time God blew your socks off when He turned your ugliness into something so beautiful that it was beyond anything you could have ever envisioned? Whenever that was, hang on to that memory and let it be your reminder that God keeps His promises. So what ugliness has invaded your life? Whatever it is, my prayer for us is that we would hold steady and wait out the ugliness with great anticipation of the beauty God has in store for us.

Heavenly Father, thank You that we can have the assurance that You will take the ugly and in its appropriate time, turn it into something beautiful. Amen.

139...THIS IS HOW I FIGHT MY BATTLES

Good morning! I am so thankful for all the ways God speaks to us. True, He speaks to us through Scripture but that is just one of many ways. Just yesterday, He spoke to me through flowers from a friend, Godly counsel from a fellow Believer, the nickering of horses at my fence, and through the lyrics of a song.

Do you ever feel like the weight of the world is coming down all around you? It seems as though you're being attacked from every side. It's like Satan is working overtime to disrupt what God wants you to do. There's a song by Michael W. Smith called *Surrounded*. I've listened to this song so much lately that I woke up singing it this morning. What a great reminder to start the day. No matter what is thrown at us through the course of this day, God wants to fight our battles. Even if you feel those fiery arrows coming at you from every direction, we need to remember that as Believers, we are surrounded by God. The song says, "It may look like I'm surrounded but I'm surrounded by You." Acknowledging that God is there with us TOTALLY changes our perspective on the issue. Michael W. Smith wrote this song using the verse found in Isaiah 61:3. The first words of the song are...

> "For the spirit of heaviness
> Put on the garment of praise
> That's how we fight our battles ..."

Do you have any battles in your life? If so, start praising the Lord for who He is and what He's already done in your life. Thank Him for all the blessings He has showered you with and for the amazing truth that He is ALWAYS with you. Praising God will release any anxiety or worry you might have as the result of your battle. Praising Him makes your insurmountable battle seem small, in comparison. So just like the song says, this is how I fight my battles. How about you?

Lord, thank You for always being right there with us. Amen.

140...PRAY FIRST

Good morning! Yesterday I had my storm shelter moved from my old house to my new one. It was quite an amazing process to watch. These guys sure knew what they were doing. I think it would be fair to say that they are experts at securing storm shelters. In the middle of a severe storm, you're glad that an expert installed your safety net. Last night as I was watching the weather, it looked like I got the shelter installed at the right time.

One of the reasons storm shelters are so effective is because we usually have a warning that severe weather or tornadoes are coming. But what about all those emotional and spiritual storms that pop up in life? What expert do you turn to as you ride out the storm? Two days ago as I was working to get the garage ready for the shelter to be moved in, I put my phone on the hood of my car so I could hear it while I was in the garage. I needed to run to the farm to get one more measurement on the shelter. When I got home, I couldn't find my phone. I looked everywhere and then got back into my car and retraced my steps. Still no phone. I started to panic but then I prayed. To make a long story short, my sister was able to locate my phone by tracking it with a Find My Phone app. It was located at the end of my street. It had fallen off the hood of my car.

I don't know if you caught this or not but I panicked before I prayed. That's as crazy as if I chose to stand outside of the storm shelter during a tornado. Psalm 46:1 says, "God is our refuge and strength, a very present help in trouble." God is always right there to be our Helper in times of trouble, regardless of how intense your trouble may be. Big or small, God wants to handle them all. And in case you hadn't heard, God is the only true Expert in life! So, here's to turning to Him first when a call of distress rings out in your life.

Lord, when trouble comes, let us be wise enough
to turn to You first. Amen.

141...SEASONS OF LIFE

Good morning! As I stepped outside this morning, I was greeted with much cooler air. It felt more like spring than summer. As I sat outside on my patio soaking it all in, I started thinking about seasons in life. We all know about the weather seasons but Genesis 50:15-21 gives us a great example of relational seasons. In these verses, Joseph's brothers were afraid of him now that their father had died. They said in verse 15, "What if Joseph bears a grudge against us and pays us back in full for all the wrong which we did to him!" In the flesh, Joseph would have been justified in repaying his brothers for the injustice that was done to him. But thankfully we are given the example of how God wants us to handle the situations of injustice in our lives. When Joseph's brothers came to him, Joseph said, "Do not be afraid, for am I in God's place? As for you, you meant evil against me, but God meant it for good in order to bring about this present result..." Joseph was wise enough to know that just letting the wrong go and allowing God to handle it was the best way to honor Him. What I love the most in verse 20 is that Joseph understood that God allowed those injustices "in order to bring about this present result."

Are you suffering injustices as a result of relationships? I think we all have at some point in our life, but did we handle it as wisely as Joseph did? It had to be so hard for Joseph to wrap his mind around the fact that his own brothers would do those things to him. But Joseph went on with his life like God expects us to do and allowed God to handle it. Someone I love dearly recently sent me a text that said, "Family are those who make a choice to be involved in being a positive part of your life." I love that definition! Joseph made the choice to be a positive part of his brother's lives. In verse 21 Joseph said, "So therefore, do not be afraid; I will provide for you and your little ones." I'm sure Joseph's brothers were relieved to hear those words, and once spoken, Joseph and his brothers entered into a new season of life.

Lord, thank You for this example of forgiveness.
Amen.

142...WHAT A DAY IT WILL BE

Good morning! My brother and sister in-law spent the weekend at my new place. It was nice having the company. They were in town to attend my brother's high school reunion. It's hard to believe that it's been forty years since he graduated high school. They really enjoyed meeting up with his classmates and catching up on each other's lives. It sounded like a really nice reunion for them all. As they were out doing their thing with his classmates, I started thinking about a reunion that I cannot wait for, and no it's not my 40th reunion coming up next year. As a matter of fact, it's not even a reunion on earth.

1 Thessalonians 4:13–18 says this:

> *But we do not want you to be uninformed, brethren, about those who are asleep, so that you will not grieve as do the rest who have no hope. For if we believe that Jesus died and rose again, even so God will bring with Him those who have fallen asleep in Jesus. For this we say to you by the word of the Lord, that we who are alive and remain until the coming of the Lord, will not precede those who have fallen asleep. For the Lord Himself will descend from heaven with a shout, with the voice of the archangel and with the trumpet of God, and the dead in Christ will rise first. Then we who are alive and remain will be caught up together with them in the clouds to meet the Lord in the air, and so we shall always be with the Lord. Therefore comfort one another with these words.*

Do you long to be with those fellow Believers who have already died and are with the Lord? I know I do. I often find myself daydreaming about it. But as much as I yearn to see those family and friends, what I really can't wait for is to be physically present with Jesus. Now that's a reunion worth me dreaming about. How about you?

Lord, what an amazing day it will be when we see You face to face. Jesus, I so long for that day, but for now, I can only dream about it. Come quickly, Lord Jesus. Amen.

143...HIS OUTSTRETCHED HAND

Good morning! Our area got hammered with lots of rain and strong winds yesterday, but thankfully no tornadoes. As I was reading about Jesus walking on water in Matthew 14, I came across the way they described the reason for the waves battering the boat the disciples were in. It says in verse 24 that "the wind was contrary." Yep, that's a good way to describe our wind yesterday that caused me to chase down the cover to my BBQ grill through my backyard … contrary, indeed!

That was just a tiny bit of information that I could relate to but the real point the Lord wanted me to see again this morning was found a few verses later in Peter's response to Jesus walking on water. We find Peter's reaction in verses 28-31. Peter said to Him, "Lord, if it is You, command me to come to You on the water." And He said, "Come!" And Peter got out of the boat, and walked on the water and came toward Jesus. But seeing the wind, he became frightened, and beginning to sink, he cried out, "Lord, save me!" Immediately Jesus stretched out His hand and took hold of him, and said to him, "You of little faith, why did you doubt?"

Peter isn't alone in that department. So, why do we doubt? The same reason Peter did. We take our eyes off the Lord and put them on our circumstances instead. How many times do we do that each day? For me, way too many. But at least when I start to sink, I realize faster what I'm doing and reach back up for the Lord's hand. And He is always there ready to pull me up so I don't drown. Do you have circumstances in your life that are pulling your eyes away from the Lord? Just like with Peter's example, when we put our attention on them instead of God, we sink. Maybe not in water like Peter but we still sink in the grips of fear, despair, depression, loneliness, etc. The good news is that once we refocus our attention on the Lord, those grips release and Jesus sustains us. Don't know about you, but I really needed that reminder.

Lord, thank You for Your constant outstretched hand! Amen.

144...WALK WORTHY

Good morning! I was flipping through Facebook last night and came across a friend's vacation pictures of her family's trip to the beach. They had left a note for the next person to see in the sand. I started thinking about the imprint that they left in the sand when they walked off from the message they left. We are all going to leave an imprint when we leave, whether that is leaving people or leaving this earth. What will your impact be when you're gone? I guess that answer depends on two questions. Were you a Believer of Jesus? And did you live life like you belonged to Him?

In Ephesians 4:1-3, Paul talks about how we should live as Believers.

> *Therefore I, the prisoner of the Lord, implore you to walk in a manner worthy of the calling with which you have been called, with all humility and gentleness, with patience, showing tolerance for one another in love, being diligent to preserve the unity of the Spirit in the bond of peace.*

Once we have accepted Jesus as our Lord and Savior, we have a new purpose in life. It is no longer acceptable to meander here and there with no real direction for our life.

Everyone will leave an imprint in the lives of the people they have crossed paths with. So, what type of an imprint, or influence, will you leave? When people are around you, are they experiencing Jesus? Do you leave them with encouragement that has been imprinted on their hearts? Do you leave a faith-legacy behind you? Do you leave a Christ-centered example of how to live the successful life or a self-centered one? Is the reason for your hope and joy evident to those in your circle of influence, no matter how big or small that circle is? If you don't like the answers you gave to any of those questions, the Good News is that there is still time to change

your responses and today would be a great day to start changing your imprint. If you are wanting that change, God the Father, Christ Jesus the Son, and the Holy Spirit are eager to help you do just that.

Lord, help us walk in a manner worthy of You. Amen.

145...IT'S WHAT WE HAVE THAT MATTERS

Good morning! God has shown me some valuable life lessons through the horses behind my house. The owner of the horses recently reduced their numbers. It upset me when I realized that many of the horses where no longer there. After a day or two of being sad over the ones gone, the Lord challenged me on that. You see, I was focusing on what I didn't have instead of giving God the glory for what I still had. And when I cleared my head and started to thank God for the blessings I enjoy from the horses that remained, I was able to see that four of the horses I had grown attached to were still there ... Smokey and Cocoa, Hugs and Legs and four others, which I haven't named yet. (By the way, Hugs is the horse on the front cover of this book.)

How often in life do we do exactly what I did with the horses ... focus on what we don't have instead of what we are blessed with? This has been a problem for us since the fall of Adam and Eve in the Garden of Eden. Genesis 2:16-17 tells us what God commanded Adam. "From any tree of the garden you may eat freely; but from the tree of knowledge of good and evil you shall not eat, for in the day that you eat from it you will surely die." We know how that story ends. The serpent, aka the enemy, convinced Eve, who then convinced Adam to eat from the only tree God told them not to eat from. And once they did, the separation between God and man began, impacting all mankind.

Why is it that we want what we can't have? And why can't we be content with what we do have? I'm sure those questions have been asked throughout every generation since Adam and Eve but they are questions worth answering. It just like what I did with the horses. For a couple of days I was bummed out over the fourteen horses that were taken to new homes instead of thanking God for the eight that remained. My prayer for us is that as God's children we would keep our focus on the blessings He has given us and thank Him often for those blessings which are truly too numerous to count.

Lord, please let us focus on what we have instead of what we don't have. Amen.

146...GOOD SAMARITAN

Good morning! I was watching a Cardinal baseball game the other day and they weren't doing so good. They've been losing quite a few games lately but the stands are still full of fans. The love for the Cardinals runs deep in the Cardinal nation. So, how do you love? Do you love through all seasons of life, ups and downs like those Cardinal fans I referred to, or are you a more fair-weather type who loves only when things are going well and people don't disappoint you or cost you anything, like your time or resources. I was thinking about this as I read Romans 12:9-13:

> *Let love be without hypocrisy. Abhor what is evil; cling to what is good. Be devoted to one another in brotherly love; give preference to one another in honor; not lagging behind in diligence, fervent in spirit, serving the Lord; rejoicing in hope, persevering in tribulation, devoted to prayer, contributing to the needs of the saints, practicing hospitality.*"

Wow! That's a tall order but a clear cut explanation of what we should do and how we should love. Of course, none of us can do any of this without the help of the Holy Spirit. Thankfully though, the Holy Spirit is right there waiting to help us love and serve others.

It's important to get loving others right. In Matthew 22:36-40, Jesus gives us the two greatest commandments: Love God with all our heart, soul and mind and love our neighbor as ourselves. In Luke 10:30-37, Jesus explains who "your neighbor" is in the parable of the Good Samaritan. This parable is a great illustration on how to show love for God and others. The Samaritan saw the need of the injured man and had compassion for him. But the part we don't always get right is what the Samaritan did next. His compassion led to action. He took the opportunity presented to help the man.

God has called us all to help those in need. But, if we are too busy and too focused just on our own stuff, then we could miss the opportunity to extend the love to others that God calls us to do. Compassion without action does about as much good as a self-centered heart that is oblivious to people hurting around them.

Lord, help us to be someone's "Good Samaritan"
today. Amen.

147...LETTING GO

Good morning! As I was waking up in my new home this morning, I was thinking about all the things that had to happen in order for the Lord to move me into this new place, which is absolutely perfect for me. And then He showed me a truth. In order to receive this incredible blessing, I had to do a lot of "letting go." Letting go of the place where Alan and I had built one memory after another. Letting go of the material things that I no longer had a place for in my smaller new home. Letting go of the provisions that Alan and I had made for each other upon either one of our deaths. And this list could go on and on. But in order for God to bless me with my new place, I had to be willing to let go of the old place. As I was reflecting on that, Ephesians 3:20-21 came to mind:

> *Now to Him who is able to do far more abundantly beyond all that we ask or think, according to the power that works within us, to Him be the glory in the church and in Christ Jesus to all generations forever and ever. Amen.*

With these verses in mind, I have a couple of questions for you today. Are you holding on to something that God is asking you to let go? Is there a blessing beyond all that you could think of or imagine that God is wanting to give you? The only way to find out is to trust Him and let go of what you currently have. Even though my house at the farm was a really good house for me, God knew that for so many reasons my new home would work much better for me. I never would have experienced this blessing if I hadn't let go of the farm and placed my trust in God, knowing He knew what was best. In order to trust the Lord, you have to have a relationship with Him. If you haven't yet accepted Jesus as your Lord and Savior, why not make that decision today? To experience His blessings that are truly beyond anything you can image, and secure for yourself a forever home in Heaven, just ask Jesus to come into your heart and to forgive you of your sins. It's just that easy. My prayer is that we would have the courage to do exactly that. Just let go and let God be God!

Lord, help anyone that doesn't know You as Lord make that decision today. And thank You for helping me complete another devotional. May You receive all the glory! Amen.

Linda Estes has mastered the one minute devotional!

Henry Neufeld
Owner
Energion Publications

"My choice was reduced, then, not to whether I'd be a caregiver, but more what kind of caregiver I'd be."

– Robert Martin

More from Energion Publications

Personal Study

Finding My Way in Christianity	Herold Weiss	$16.99
The Jesus Paradigm	David Alan Black	$17.99
When People Speak for God	Henry Neufeld	$17.99

Christian Living

Faith in the Public Square	Robert D. Cornwall	$16.99
Grief: Finding the Candle of Light	Jody Neufeld	$8.99
Directed Paths	Myrtle Neufeld	$9.99
Pathways to Prayer	David Moffett-Moore	$5.99

Bible Study

Learning and Living Scripture	Lentz/Neufeld	$12.99
Luke: A Participatory Study Guide	Geoffrey Lentz	$8.99
Philippians: A Participatory Study Guide	Bruce Epperly	$9.99
Ephesians: A Participatory Study Guide	Robert D. Cornwall	$9.99
Meditations on According to John	Herold Weiss	$14.99
The Jesus Manifesto	David Moffett-Moore	$9.99
Those Footnotes in Your Bible	Thomas W. Hudgins	$5.99

Theology

Creation in Scripture	Herold Weiss	$12.99
Creation: the Christian Doctrine	Edward W. H. Vick	$12.99
Ultimate Allegiance	Robert D. Cornwall	$9.99
The Journey to the Undiscovered Country	William Powell Tuck	$9.99
From Here to Eternity	Bruce Epperly	$5.99

Ministry

Clergy Table Talk	Kent Ira Groff	$9.99
So Much Older Then …	Robert LaRochelle	$9.99
Wind and Whirlwind	David Moffett-Moore	$9.99
A Positive Word for Christian Lamenting	William Powell Tuck	$16.99

Generous Quantity Discounts Available
Dealer Inquiries Welcome
Energion Publications — P.O. Box 841
Gonzalez, FL 32560
Website: http://energionpubs.com
Phone: (850) 525-3916

CPSIA information can be obtained
at www.ICGtesting.com
Printed in the USA
FSHW012339071118

9 781631 996160